THE SURPRISING ADVENTU
WITH THOSE OF GENERAL ⸺ ⸺AN
IMPROVING HISTORY FOR O⸺ ⸺UNG BOYS,
GOOD BOYS, BAD BOYS, BIG ⸺YS, LITTLE BOYS,
COW BOYS, AND TOM-BOYS

BY

S. R. Crockett

THE SURPRISING ADVENTURES OF SIR TOADY LION WITH THOSE OF GENERAL NAPOLEON SMITH : AN IMPROVING HISTORY FOR OLD BOYS, YOUNG BOYS, GOOD BOYS, BAD BOYS, BIG BOYS, LITTLE BOYS, COW BOYS, AND TOM-BOYS

Published by Dossier Press

New York City, NY

First published circa 1914

ABOUT DOSSIER PRESS

Since the moment people have been writing, they've been writing non-fiction works, from the *Histories* of Herodotus to the Code of Hammurabi. **Dossier Press** publishes all of the classic non-fiction works ever written and makes them available to new and old readers alike at the touch of a button.

CHAPTER I.

PRISSY, HUGH JOHN, AND SIR TOADY LION.

IT is always difficult to be great, but it is specially difficult when greatness is thrust upon one, as it were, along with the additional burden of a distinguished historical name. This was the case with General Napoleon Smith. Yet when this story opens he was not a general. That came later, along with the cares of empire and the management of great campaigns.

But already in secret he was Napoleon Smith, though his nurse sometimes still referred to him as Johnnie, and his father—but stay. I will reveal to you the secret of our soldier's life right at the start. Though a Napoleon, our hero was no Buonaparte. No, his name was Smith—plain Smith; his father was the owner of four large farms and a good many smaller ones, near that celebrated Border which separates the two hostile countries of England and Scotland. Neighbours referred to the General's father easily as "Picton Smith of Windy Standard," from the soughing, mist-nursing mountain of heather and fir-trees which gave its name to the estate, and to the large farm he had cultivated himself ever since the death of his wife, chiefly as a means of distracting his mind, and keeping at a distance loneliness and sad thoughts.

Hugh John Smith had never mentioned the fact of his Imperial descent to his father, but in a moment of confidence he had told his old nurse, who smiled with a world-weary wisdom, which betrayed her knowledge of the secrets of courts—and said that doubtless it was so. He had also a brother and sister, but they were not, at that time, of the race of the Corporal of Ajaccio. On the contrary, Arthur George, the younger, aged five, was an engine-driver. There was yet another who rode in a mail-cart, and puckered up his face upon being addressed in a strange foreign language, as "Was-it-then? A darling—goo-goo—then it was!" This creature, however, was not owned as a brother by Hugh John and Arthur George, and indeed may at this point be dismissed from the story. The former went so far as stoutly to deny his brother's sex, in the face of such proofs as were daily afforded by Baby's tendency to slap his sister's face wherever they met, and also to seize things and throw them on the floor for the pleasure of seeing them break. Arthur George, however, had secret hopes that Baby would even yet turn out a satisfactory boy whenever he saw him killing flies on the window, and on these occasions hounded him on to yet deadlier exertions. But he dared not mention his anticipations to his soldier brother, that haughty scion of an Imperial race. For reasons afterwards to be given, Arthur George was usually known as Toady Lion.

Then Hugh John had a sister. Her name was Priscilla. Priscilla was distinguished also, though not in a military sense. She was literary, and wrote books "on the sly," as Hugh John said. He considered this secrecy the only respectable part of a very shady business. Specially he objected to being made to serve as the hero of Priscilla's tales, and went so far as to promise to "thump" his sister if he caught her introducing him as of any military rank under that of either general or colour-sergeant.

"Look here, Pris," he said on one occasion, "if you put me into your beastly girl books all about dolls and love and trumpery, I'll bat you over the head with a wicket!"

"Hum—I dare say, if you could catch me," said Priscilla, with her nose very much in the air.

"Catch you! I'll catch and bat you now if you say much."

"Much, much! Can't, can't! There! 'Fraid cat! Um-m-um!"

"By Jove, then, I just will!"

It is sad to be obliged to state here, in the very beginning of these veracious chronicles, that at this time Prissy and Napoleon Smith were by no means model children, though Prissy afterwards marvellously improved. Even their best friends admitted as much, and as for their enemies— well, their old gardener's remarks when they chased each other over his newly planted beds would be out of place even in a military periodical, and might be the means of preventing a book with Mr. Gordon Browne's nice pictures from being included in some well-conducted Sunday-school libraries.

General Napoleon Smith could not catch Priscilla (as, indeed, he well knew before he started), especially when she picked up her skirts and went right at hedges and ditches like a young colt. Napoleon looked upon this trait in Prissy's character as degrading and unsportsmanlike in the extreme. He regarded long skirts, streaming hair, and flapping, aggravating pinafores as the natural handicap of girls in the race of life, and as particularly useful when they "cheeked" their brothers. It was therefore wicked to neutralise these equalising disadvantages by strings tied round above the knees, or by the still more scientific device of a sash suspended from the belt before, passed between Prissy's legs, and attached to the belt behind.

But, then, as Napoleon admitted even at ten years of age, girls are capable of anything; and to his dying day he has never had any reason to change his opinion—at least, so far as he has yet got.

"All right, then, I will listen to your old stuff if you will say you are sorry, and promise to be my horse, and let me lick you for an hour afterwards—besides giving me a penny."

It was thus that Priscilla, to whom in after times great lights of criticism listened with approval, was compelled to stoop to artifice and bribery in order to secure and hold her first audience. Whereupon the authoress took paper from her pocket, and as she did so, held the manuscript with its back to Napoleon Smith, in order to conceal the suspicious shortness of the lines. But that great soldier instantly detected the subterfuge.

"It's a penny more for listening to poetry!" he said, with sudden alacrity.

"I know it is," replied Prissy sadly, "but you might be nice about it just this once. I'm dreadfully, dreadfully poor this week, Hugh John!"

"So am I," retorted Napoleon Smith sternly; "if I wasn't, do you think I would listen at all to your beastly old poetry? Drive on!"

Thus encouraged, Priscilla meekly began—

"My love he is a soldier bold, And my love is a knight; He girds him in a coat of mail, When he goes forth to fight."

"That's not quite so bad as usual," said Napoleon condescendingly, toying meanwhile with the lash of an old dog-whip he had just "boned" out of the harness-room. Priscilla beamed gratefully upon her critic, and proceeded—

"He rides him forth across the sand——"

"Who rides whom?" cried Napoleon. "Didn't the fool ride a horse?"

"It means himself," said Priscilla meekly.

"Then why doesn't it say so?" cried the critic triumphantly, tapping his boot with the "boned" dog-whip just like any ordinary lord of creation in presence of his inferiors.

"It's poetry," explained Priscilla timidly.

"It's silly!" retorted Napoleon, judicially and finally.

Priscilla resumed her reading in a lower and more hurried tone. She knew that she was skating over thin ice.

"He rides him forth across the sand, Upon a stealthy steed."

"You mean 'stately,' you know," interrupted Napoleon—somewhat rudely, Priscilla thought. Yet he was quite within his rights, for Priscilla had not yet learned that a critic always knows what you mean to say much better than you do yourself.

"No, I don't mean 'stately,'" said Priscilla, "I mean 'stealthy,' the way a horse goes on sand. You go and gallop on the sea-shore and you'll find out."

I've listened quite a pennyworth now."

"He rides him forth across the sand, Upon a stealthy steed, And when he sails upon the sea, He plays upon a reed!"

"Great soft he was," cried Napoleon Smith; "and if ever I hear you say that I did such a thing——"

Priscilla hurried on more quickly than ever.

"In all the world there's none can do The deeds that he hath done: When he hath slain his enemies, Then he comes back alone."

"That's better!" said Napoleon, nodding encouragement. "At any rate it isn't long. Now, give me my penny."

"Shan't," said Priscilla, the pride of successful achievement swelling in her breast; "besides, it isn't Saturday yet, and you've only listened to three verses anyway. You will have to listen to ever so much more than that before you get a penny."

"Hugh John! Priscilla!" came a voice from a distance.

The great soldier Napoleon Smith instantly effected a retreat in masterly fashion behind a gooseberry bush.

"There's Jane calling us," said Priscilla; "she wants us to go in and be washed for dinner."

"Course she does," sneered Napoleon; "think she's out screeching like that for fun? Well, let her. I am not going in to be towelled till I'm all over red and scurfy, and get no end of soap in my eyes."

"But Jane wants you; she'll be so cross if you don't come."

"I don't care for Jane," said Napoleon Smith with dignity, but all the same making himself as small as possible behind his gooseberry bush.

"But if you don't come in, Jane will tell father——"

"I don't care for father—" the prone but gallant General was proceeding to declare in the face of Priscilla's horrified protestations that he mustn't speak so, when a slow heavy step was heard on the other side of the hedge, and a deep voice uttered the single syllable, "John!"

"Yes, father," a meek young man standing up behind the gooseberry bush instantly replied: he was trying to brush himself as clean as circumstances would permit. "Yes, father; were you calling me, father?"

Incredible as it seems, the meek and apologetic words were those of that bold enemy of tyrants, General Napoleon Smith.

Priscilla smiled at the General as he emerged from the hands of Jane, "red and scurfy," just as he had said. She smiled meaningly and aggravatingly, so that Napoleon was reduced to shaking his clenched fist covertly at her.

"Wait till I get you out," he said, using the phrase time-honoured by such occasions.

Priscilla Smith only smiled more meaningly still. "First catch your hare!" she said under her breath.

Napoleon Smith stalked in to lunch, the children's dinner at the house of Windy Standard, with an expression of fixed and Byronic gloom on his face, which was only lightened by the sight of his favourite pigeon-pie (with a lovely crust) standing on the side-board.

"Say grace, Hugh John," commanded his father.

And General Napoleon Smith said grace with all the sweet innocence of a budding angel singing in the cherub choir, aiming at the same time a kick at his sister underneath the table, which overturned a footstool and damaged the leg of a chair.

CHAPTER II

THE GOSPEL OF DASHT-MEAN.

IT was on the day preceding a great review near the Border town of Edam, that Hugh John Picton Smith first became a soldier and a Napoleon. His father's house was connected by a short avenue with a great main road along which king and beggar had for a thousand years gone posting to town. Now the once celebrated highway lies deserted, for along the heights to the east run certain bars of metal, shining and parallel, over which rush all who can pay the cost of a third-class ticket—a roar like thunder preceding them, white steam and sulphurous reek wreathing after them. The great highway beneath is abandoned to the harmless impecunious bicyclist, and on the North Road the sweeping cloud dust has it all its own way.

But Hugh John loved the great thoroughfare, deserted though it was. To his mind there could be no loneliness upon its eye-taking stretches, for who knew but out of the dust there might come with a clatter Mr. Dick Turpin, late of York and Tyburn; Robert the Bruce, charging south into England with his Galloway garrons, to obtain some fresh English beef wherewithal to feed his scurvy Scots; or (best of all) his Majesty King George's mail-coach Highflyer, the picture of which, coloured and blazoned, hung in his father's workroom.

People told him that all these great folks were long since dead. But Hugh John knew better than to believe any "rot" grown-ups might choose to palm off on him. What did grown-ups know anyway? They were rich, of course. Unlimited shillings were at their command; and as for pennies—well, all the pennies in the world lived in their breeches' pockets. But what use did they make of these god-like gifts? Did you ever meet them at the tuck-shop down in the town buying fourteen cheese-cakes for a shilling, as any sensible person would? Did they play with "real-real trains," drawn by locomotives of shining brass? No! they preferred either one lump of sugar or none at all in their tea. This showed how much they knew about what was good for them.

So if such persons informed him that Robert the Bruce had been dead some time, or showed him the rope with which Turpin was hung, coiled on a pedestal in a horrid dull museum (free on Saturdays, 10 to 4), Hugh John Picton looked and nodded, for he was an intelligent boy. If you didn't nod sometimes as if you were taking it all in, they would explain it all over again to you— with abominable dates and additional particulars, which they would even ask you afterwards if you remembered.

"MR. DICK TURPIN, LATE OF YORK AND TYBURN."

For many years Hugh John had gone every day down to the porter's lodge at the end of the avenue, and though old Betty the rheumaticky warder was not allowed to let him out, he stared happily enough through the bars. It was a white gate of strong wood, lovely to swing on if you happened to be there when it was opened for a carriageful of calling-folk in the afternoon, or for Hugh John's father when he went out a-riding.

But you had to hide pretty quick behind the laurels, and rush out in that strictly limited period before old Betty found her key, and yet after the tail of Agincourt, his father's great grey horse, had switched round the corner. If you were the least late, Betty would get ahead of you, and the gates of Paradise would be shut. If you were a moment too soon, it was just as bad—or even worse. For then the voice of "He-whom-it-was-decidedly-most-healthy-to-obey" would sound up the road, commanding instant return to the Sandheap or the High Garden.

So on these occasions Hugh John mostly brought Sir Toady Lion with him—otherwise Arthur George the Sturdy, and at yet other times variously denominated Prince Murat, the Old Guard, the mob that was scattered with the whiff of grapeshot, and (generally) the whole Grand Army of the First Empire. Toady Lion (his own first effort at the name of his favourite hero Richard Cœur-de-Lion) had his orders, and with guile and blandishments held Betty in check till the last frisk of Agincourt's tail had disappeared round the corner. Then Hugh John developed his plans of assault, and was soon swinging on the gate.

"Out of the way with you, Betty," he would cry, "or you will get hurt—sure."

For the white gate shut of itself, and you had only to push it open, jump on, check it at the proper place on the return journey, and with your foot shove off again to have scores and scores of lovely swings. Then Betty would go up the avenue and shout for her husband, who was the aforesaid crusty old gardener. She would have laid down her life for Toady Lion, but by no means even a part of it for Hugh John, which was unfair. Old Betty had once been upset by the slam of the gate on a windy day, and so was easily intimidated by the shouts of the horseman and the appalling motion of his white five-barred charger.

Such bliss, however, was transient, and might have to be expiated in various ways—at best with a slap from the hand of Betty (which was as good as nothing at all), at worst, by a visit to father's workroom—which could not be thought upon without a certain sense of solemnity, as if Sunday had turned up once too often in the middle of the week.

But upon this great day of which I have to tell, Hugh John had been honourably digging all the morning in the sand-hole. He had on his red coat, which was his most secret pride, and he was devising a still more elaborate system of fortification. Bastion and trench, scarp and counter-scarp, lunette and ravelenta (a good word), Hugh John had made them all, and he was now besieging his own creation with the latest thing in artillery, calling "Boom!" when he fired off his cannon, and "Bang-whack!" as often as the projectile hit the wall and brought down a foot of the noble fortification, lately so laboriously constructed and so tenderly patted into shape.

Suddenly there came a sound which always made the heart of Hugh John beat in his side. It was the low thrilling reverberation of the drum. He had only time to dash for his cap, which he had filled with sand and old nails in order to "be a bomb-shell"; empty it, put it on his head, gird on his London sword-with-the-gold-hilt, and fly.

As he ran down the avenue the shrill fifes kept stinging his ears and making him feel as if needles were running up and down his back. It was at this point that Hugh John had a great struggle with himself. Priscilla and Toady Lion were playing at "House" and "Tea-parties" under the weeping elm on the front lawn. It was a debasing taste, certainly, but after all blood was thicker than water. And—well, he could not bear that they should miss the soldiers. But then, on the other hand, if he went back the troops might be past before he reached the gate, and Betty, he knew well, would not let him out to run after them, and the park wall was high.

In this desperate strait Hugh John called all the resources of religion to his aid.

"It would," he said, "be dasht-mean to go off without telling them."

Hugh John did not know exactly what "dasht-mean" meant. But he had heard his cousin Fred (who was grown up, had been a year at school, and wore a tall hat on Sundays) tell how all the fellows said that it was better to die-and-rot than to be "dasht-mean"; and also how those who in spite of warnings proved themselves "dasht-mean" were sent to a place called Coventry—which from all accounts seemed to be a "dasht-mean" locality.

So Hugh John resolved that he would never get sent there, and whenever a little thing tugged down in his stomach and told him "not to," Hugh John said, "Hang it! I won't be dasht-mean."— And wasn't.

Grown-ups call these things conscience and religion; but this is how it felt to Hugh John, and it answered just as well—or even better.

So when the stinging surge of distant pipes sent the wild blood coursing through his veins, and he felt his face grow cold and prickly all over, Napoleon Smith started to run down the avenue. He could not help it. He must see the soldiers or die. But all the same Tug-tug went the little string remorselessly in his stomach.

"I must see them. I must—I must!" he cried, arguing with himself and trying to drown the inner voice.

"Tug-tug-tug!" went the string, worse than that which he once put round his toe and hung out of the window, for Tom Cannon the under-keeper to wake him with at five in the morning to go rabbit-ferreting.

Hugh John turned towards the house and the weeping elm.

"It's a blooming shame," he said, "and they won't care anyway. But I can't be dasht-mean!"

And so he ran with all his might back to the weeping elm, and with a warning cry set Prissy and Sir Toady Lion on the alert. Then with anxious tumultuous heart, and legs almost as invisible as the twinkling spokes of a bicycle, so quickly did they pass one another, Hugh John fairly flung himself in the direction of the White Gate.

CHAPTER III

HOW HUGH JOHN BECAME GENERAL NAPOLEON.

EVEN dull Betty had heard the music. The White Gate was open, and with a wild cry Hugh John sprang through. Betty had a son in the army, and her deaf old ears were quickened by the fife and drum.

"Come back, Master Hugh!" she cried, as he passed through and stood on the roadside, just as the head of the column, marching easily, turned the corner of the White Road and came dancing and undulating towards him. Hugh John's heart danced also. It was still going fast with running so far; but at sight of the soldiers it took a new movement, just like little waves on a lake when they jabble in the wind, so nice and funny when you feel it—tickly too—down at the bottom of your throat.

The first who came were soldiers in a dark uniform with very stern, bearded officers, who attended finely to discipline, for they were about to enter the little town of Edam, which lay just below the white gates of Windy Standard.

So intently they marched that no one cast a glance at Hugh John standing with his drawn sword, giving the salute which his friend Sergeant Steel had taught him as each company passed. Not that Hugh John cared, or even knew that they did not see him. They were the crack volunteer regiment of the Grey City beyond the hills, and their standard of efficiency was something tremendous.

Then came red-coats crowned with helmets, red-coats tipped with Glengarry bonnets, and one or two brass bands of scattering volunteer regiments. Hugh John saluted them all. No one paid the least attention to him. He did not indeed expect any one to notice him—a small dusty boy with a sword too big for him standing at the end of the road under the shadow of the elms. Why should these glorious creations deign to notice him—shining blades, shouldered arms, flashing bayonets, white pipe-clayed belts? Were they not as gods, knowing good and evil?

But all the same he saluted every one of them impartially as they came, and the regiments swung past unregarding, dust-choked, and thirsty.

Then at last came the pipes and the waving tartans. Something cracked in Hugh John's throat, and he gave a little cry, so that his old nurse, Janet Sheepshanks, anxious for his welfare, came to take him away. But he struck at her—his own dear Janet—and fled from her grasp to the other side of the road, where he was both safer and nearer to the soldiers. Swinging step, waving plumes, all in review order on came the famous regiment, every man stepping out with a trained elasticity which went to the boy's heart. Thus and not otherwise the Black Watch followed their pipers. Hugh John gave a long sigh when they had passed, and the pipes dulled down the dusky glade.

Then came more volunteers, and yet more and more. Would they never end? And ever the sword of Hugh John Picton flashed to the salute, and his small arm waxed weary as it rose and fell.

Then happened the most astonishing thing in the world, the greatest event of Hugh John's life.

For there came to his ear a new sound, the clatter of cavalry hoofs. A bugle rang out, and Hugh John's eyes watched with straining eagerness the white dust rise and swirl behind the columns. Perhaps—who knows?—this was his reward for not being dasht-mean! But now Hugh John had forgotten Prissy and Toady Lion, father and nurse alike, heaven, earth—and everything else. There was no past for him. He was the soldier of all time. His dusty red coat and his flashing sword were the salute of the universal spirit of man to the god of war—also other fine things of which I have no time to write.

For the noble grey horses, whose predecessors Napoleon had watched so wistfully at Waterloo, came trampling along, tossing their heads with an obvious sense of their own worth as a spectacle. Hugh John paled to the lips at sight of them, but drew himself more erect than ever. He had seen foot-soldiers and volunteers before, but never anything like this.

On they came, a fine young fellow leading them, sitting carelessly on the noblest charger of all. Perhaps he was kindly by nature. Perhaps he had a letter from his sweetheart in his breastpocket. Perhaps—but it does not matter, at any rate he was young and happy, as he sat erect, leading the "finest troop in the finest regiment in the world." He saw the small dusty boy in the red coat under the elm-trees. He marked his pale twitching face, his flashing eye, his erect carriage, his soldierly port. The fate of Hugh John stood on tiptoe. He had never seen any being so glorious as this. He could scarce command himself to salute. But though he trembled in every limb, and his under lip "wickered" strangely, the hand which held the sword was steady, and went through the beautiful movements of the military salute which Sergeant Steel of the Welsh Fusiliers had taught him, with exactness and decorum.

The young officer smiled. His own hand moved to the response almost involuntarily, as if Hugh John had been one of his own troopers.

The boy's heart stood still. Could this thing be? A real soldier had saluted him!

"IT COULD NOT HAVE BEEN BETTER DONE FOR A FIELD-MARSHAL."

But there was something more marvellous yet to come. A sweet spring of good deeds welled up in that young officer's breast. Heaven speed him (as doubtless it will) in his wooing, and make him ere his time a general, with the Victoria Cross upon his breast. But though (as I hope) he rise to be Commander-in-Chief, he will never do a prettier action than that day, when the small grimy boy stood under the elm-trees at the end of the avenue of Windy Standard. This is what he did. He turned about in his saddle.

"Attention, men, draw swords!" he cried, and his voice rang like a trumpet, so grand it was—at least so Hugh John thought.

There came a glitter of unanimous steel as the swords flashed into line. The horses tossed their heads at the stirring sound, and jingled their accoutrements as the men gathered their bridle reins up in their left hands.

"Eyes right! Carry swords!" came again the sharp command.

And every blade made an arc of glittering light as it came to the salute. It could not have been better done for a field-marshal.

No fuller cup of joy was ever drunk by mortal. The tears welled up in Hugh John's eyes as he stood there in the pride of the honour done to him. To be knighted was nothing to this. He had been acknowledged as a soldier by the greatest soldier there. Hugh John did not doubt that this glorious being was he who had led the Greys in the charge at Waterloo. Who else could have done that thing?

He was no longer a little dusty boy. He stood there glorified, ennobled. The world was almost too full.

"Eyes front! Slope swords!" rang the words once more.

The pageant passed by. Only the far drum-throb came back as he stood speechless and motionless, till his father rode up on his way home, and seeing the boy asked him what he was doing there. Then for all reply a little clicking hitch came suddenly in his throat. He wanted to laugh, but somehow instead the tears ran down his cheeks, and he gasped out a word or two which sounded like somebody else's voice.

"I'm not hurt, father," he said, "I'm not crying. It was only that the Scots Greys saluted me. And I can't help it, father. It goes tick-tick in my throat, and I can't keep it back. But I'm not crying, father! I'm not indeed!"

Then the stern man gathered the great soldier up and set him across his saddle—for Hugh John was alone, the others having long ago gone back with Janet Sheepshanks. And his father did not say anything, but let him sit in front with the famous sword in his hands which had brought about such strange things. And even thus rode our hero home—Hugh John Picton no more, but rather General Napoleon Smith; nor shall his rank be questioned on any army roster of strong unblenching hearts.

But late that night Hugh John stole down the hushed avenue, his bare feet pattering through the dust which the dew was making cool. He climbed the gate and stood under the elm, with the wind flapping his white nightgown like a battle flag. Then clasping his hands, he took the solemn binding oath of his religion, "The Scots Greys saluted me. May I die-and-rot if ever I am dasht-mean again!"

CHAPTER IV

CASTLE PERILOUS.

IN one corner of the property of Hugh John's father stood an ancient castle—somewhat doubtfully of it, however, for it was claimed as public property by the adjoining abbey town, now much decayed and fallen from its high estate, but desirous of a new lease of life as a tourist and manufacturing centre. The castle and the abbey had for centuries been jealous neighbours, treacherous friends, embattled enemies according to the fluctuating power of those who possessed them. The lord of the castle harried the abbot and his brethren. The abbot promptly retaliated by launching, in the name of the Church, the dread ban of excommunication against the freebooter. The castle represented feudal rights, the abbey popular and ecclesiastical authority.

And so it was still. Mr. Picton Smith had, indeed, only bought the property a few years before the birth of our hero; but, among other encumbrances, he had taken over a lawsuit with the town concerning the castle, which for years had been dragging its slow length along. Edam Abbey was a show-place of world-wide repute, and the shillings of the tourist constituted a very important item in the finances of the overburdened municipality. If the Council and magistrates of the good town of Edam could add the Castle of Windy Standard to their attractions, the resultant additional sixpence a head would go far towards making up the ancient rental of the town parks, which now let for exactly half of their former value.

But Mr. Picton Smith was not minded thus tamely to hand over an ancient fortress, secured to him by deed and charter. He declared at once that he would resist the claims of the town by every means in his power. He would, however, refuse right-of-way to no respectable sightseer. The painter, all unchallenged, might set up his easel there, the poet meditate, even the casual wanderer in search of the picturesque and romantic, have free access to these gloomy and desolate halls. The townspeople would be at liberty to conduct their friends and visitors thither. But Mr. Smith was resolved that the ancient fortalice of the Windy Standard should not be made a vulgar show. Sandwich papers and ginger-beer bottles would not be permitted to profane the green sward of the courtyard, across which had so often ridden all the chivalry of the dead Lorraines.

"Those who want sixpenny shows will find plenty at Edam Fair," was Mr. Picton Smith's ultimatum. And when he had once committed himself, like most of his stalwart name, Mr. Smith had the reputation of being very set in his mind.

But in spite of this the town asserted its right-of-way through the courtyard. A footpath was said to have passed that way by which persons might go to and fro to kirk and market.

"I have no doubt a footpath passed through my dining-room a few centuries ago," said Mr. Smith, "but that does not compel me to keep my front and back doors open for all the rabble of Edam to come and go at their pleasure."

And forthwith he locked his lodge gates and bought the largest mastiff he could obtain. The castle stood on an island rather more than a mile long, a little below the mansion house. A wooden bridge led over the deeper, narrower, and more rapid branch of the Edam River from the direction of the abbey and town. Across the broader and shallower branch there could be traced, from the house of Windy Standard, the remains of an ancient causeway. This, in the place where the stream was to be crossed, had become a series of stepping-stones over which Hugh John and Priscilla could go at a run (without falling in and wetting themselves more than once in three or four times), but which still constituted an impregnable barrier to the short fat legs of Toady Lion—who usually stood on the shore and proclaimed his woes to the world at large till somebody carried him over and deposited him on the castle island.

Affairs were in this unsettled condition when, at twelve years of age, Hugh John ceased to be Hugh John, and became, without, however, losing his usual surname of Smith, one of the august and imperial race of the Buonapartes.

It was a clear June evening, the kind of night when the whole landscape seems to have been newly swept, washed down, and generally spring-cleaned. All nature spoke peace to Janet Sheepshanks, housekeeper, nurse, and general responsible female head of the house of Windy Standard, when a procession came towards her across the stepping-stones over the broad Edam water from the direction of the castle island. Never had such a disreputable sight presented itself to the eyes of Janet Sheepshanks. At once douce and severe, sharp-tongued and covertly affectionate, she represented the authority of a father who was frequently absent from them, and the memory of a dead mother which remained to the three children in widely different degrees. To Priscilla her mother was a loving being, gracious alike by the tender sympathy of her voice and by the magic of a touch which healed all childish troubles with the kiss of peace upon the place "to make it well." To Hugh John she had been a confidant to whom he could rush, eager and dishevelled, with the tale of the glorious defeat of some tin enemy (for even in those prehistoric days Hugh John had been a soldier), and who, smoothing back his ruffled hair, was prepared to join as eagerly as himself in all his tiny triumphs. But to Toady Lion, though he hushed the shrill persistence of his treble to a reverent murmur when he talked of "muvver," she was only an imagination, fostered mostly by Priscilla—his notion of motherhood being taken from his rough-handed loving Janet Sheepshanks; while the tomb in the village churchyard was a place to which he had no desire to accompany his mother, and from whose gloomy precincts he sought to escape as soon as possible.

CHAPTER V

THE DECLARATION OF WAR.

BUT, meanwhile, Janet Sheepshanks stands at the end of the stepping-stones, and Janet is hardly a person to keep waiting anywhere near the house of Windy Standard.

Over the stepping-stones came as leader Priscilla Smith, her head thrown back, straining in every nerve with the excitement of carrying Sir Toady Lion, whose scratched legs and shoeless feet dangled over the stream. Immediately beneath her, and wading above the knee in the rush of the water, there staggered through the shallows Hugh John, supporting his sister with voice and hand—or, as he would have said, "boosting her up" whenever she swayed riverward with her burden, pushing her behind when she hesitated, and running before to offer his back as an additional stepping-stone when the spaces were wide between the boulders.

Janet Sheepshanks waited grimly for her charges on the bank, and her eyes seemed to deceive her, words to fail her, as the children came nearer. Never had such a sight been seen near the decent house of Windy Standard. Miss Priscilla and her pinafore were represented by a ragged tinkler's lass with a still more ragged frill about her neck. Her cheeks and hands were as variously scratched as if she had fallen into a whole thicket of brambles. Her face, too, was pale, and the tatooed places showed bright scarlet against the whiteness of her skin. She had lost a shoe, and her dress was ripped to the knee by a great ragged triangular tear, which flapped wet about her ankles as she walked.

Sir Toady Lion was somewhat less damaged, but still showed manifold signs of rough usage. His lace collar, the pride of Janet Sheepshanks' heart, was torn nearly off his shoulders, and now hung jagged and unsightly down his back. Several buttons of his well-ordered tunic were gone, and as to his person he was mud as far above the knees as could be seen without turning him upside down.

"NO WONDER THAT JANET SHEEPSHANKS AWAITED THIS SORRY PROCESSION WITH A GRIM TIGHTENING OF THE LIPS."

But Hugh John—words are vain to describe the plight of Hugh John. One eye was closed, and began to be discoloured, taking on above the cheekbone the shot green and purple of a half-ripe plum. His lip was cut, and a thin thread of scarlet stealing down his brow told of a broken head. What remained of his garments presented a ruin more complete, if less respectable, than the ancient castle of the Windy Standard. Neither shoe nor shoe-string, neither stocking nor collar, remained intact upon him. On his bare legs were the marks of cruel kicks, and for ease of transport he carried the débris of his jacket under his arm. He had not the remotest idea where his cap had gone to.

No wonder that Janet Sheepshanks awaited this sorry procession with a grim tightening of the lips, or that her hand quivered with the desire of punishment, even while her kind and motherly heart yearned to be busy repairing damages and binding up the wounded. Of this feeling, however, it was imperative that for the present, in the interests of discipline, she should show nothing.

It was upon Priscilla, as the eldest in years and senior responsible officer in charge, that Janet first turned the vials of her wrath.

"Eh, Priscilla Smith, but ye are a ba-a-ad, bad lassie. Ye should ha'e your bare back slashit wi' nettles! Where ha'e ye been, and what ha'e ye done to these twa bairns? Ye shall be marched straight to your father, and if he doesna gar ye loup when ye wad raither stand still, and claw where ye are no yeuky, he will no be doing his duty to the Almichty, and to your puir mither that's lang syne in her restin' grave in the kirk-yaird o' Edom."

By which fervent address in her native tongue, Janet meant that Mr. Smith would be decidedly spoiling the child if on this occasion he spared the rod. Janet could speak good enough formal English when she chose, for instance to her master on Sabbath, or to the minister on visitation days; but whenever she was excited she returned to that vigorous ancient Early English which some miscall a dialect, and of which she had a noble and efficient command.

To Janet's attack, Priscilla answered not a word either of explanation or apology. She recognised that the case had gone far beyond that. She only set Sir Toady Lion on his feet, and bent down to brush the mud from his tunic with her usual sisterly gesture. Janet Sheepshanks thrust her aside without ceremony.

"My wee man," she said, "what have they done to you?"

Toady Lion began volubly, and in his usual shrill piping voice, to make an accusation against certain bad boys who had "hit him," and "hurted him," and "kicked him." And now when at last he was safely delivered and lodged in the well-proven arms of Janet Sheepshanks his tears flowed apace, and made clean furrows down the woebegone grubbiness of his face.

Priscilla walked by Janet's side, white and silent, nerving herself for the coming interview. At ordinary times Janet Sheepshanks was terrible enough, and her word law in all the precincts of Windy Standard. But Priscilla knew that she must now face the anger of her father; and so, with this in prospect, the railing accusations of her old nurse scarcely so much as reached her ears.

Hugh John, stripped of all military pomp, limped behind—a short, dry, cheerless sob shaking him at intervals. But in reality this was more the protest of ineffectual anger than any concession to unmanly weakness.

CHAPTER VI

FIRST BLOOD.

TEN minutes later, and without, as Jane Sheepshanks said, "so muckle as a sponge or a brush-and-comb being laid upon them," the three stood before their father. Silently Janet had introduced them, and now as silently she stood aside to listen to the evidence—and, as she put it, "keep the maister to his duty, and mind him o' his responsibilities to them that's gane."

Janet Sheepshanks never forgot that she had been maid for twenty years to the dead mother of the children, nor that she had received "the bits o' weans" at her hand as a dying charge. She considered herself, with some reason, to be the direct representative of the missing parent, and referred to Priscilla, Toady Lion, and Hugh John as "my bairns," just as, in moments of affection, she would still speak to them of "my bonnie lassie your mither," as if the dead woman were still one of her flock.

For a full minute Mr. Picton Smith gazed speechless at the spectacle before him. He had been writing something that crinkled his brow and compressed his lips, and at the patter of the children's feet in the passage outside his door, as they ceremoniously marshalled themselves to enter, he had turned about on his great office chair with a smile of expectation and anticipation. The door opened, and Janet Sheepshanks pushed in first Sir Toady Lion, still voluble and calling for vengeance on the "bad, bad boys at the castle that had striked him and hurted his dear Prissy." Priscilla herself stood white-lipped and dumb, and through the awful silence pulsed the dry, recurrent, sobbing catch in the throat of Hugh John.

Mr. Picton Smith was a stern man, whose great loss had caused him to shut up the springs of his tenderness from the world. But they flowed the sweeter and the rarer underneath; and though his grave and dignified manner daunted his children on the occasion of any notable evil-doing, they had no reason to be afraid of him.

"Well, what is the meaning of this?" he said, his face falling into a greyer and graver silence at the sound of Hugh John's sobs, and turning to Priscilla for explanation.

Meanwhile Sir Toady Lion was pursuing the subject with his usual shrill alacrity.

"Be quiet, sir," said his father. "I will hear you all one by one, but let Priscilla begin—she is the eldest."

"We went to the castle after dinner, over by the stepping-stones," began Priscilla, fingering nervously the frill of the torn pinafore about her throat, "and when we got to the castle we found out that our pet lamb Donald had come after us by the ford; and he was going everywhere about the castle, trying to rub his bell off his neck on the gate-posts and on the stones at the corners."

"Yes, and I stooded on a rock, and Donald he butted me over behind!" came the voice of Sir Toady Lion in shrill explanation of his personal share in the adventure.

"And then we played on the grass in the inside of the castle. Toady Lion and I were plaiting daisy-chains and garlands for Donald, and Hugh John was playing at being the Prisoner of Chillyon: he had tied himself to the gate-post with a rope."

"'Twasn't," muttered Hugh John, who was a stickler for accuracy; "it was a plough-chain!"

"And it rattled," added Sir Toady Lion, not to be out of the running.

"And just when we were playing nicely, a lot of horrid boys from the town came swarming and clambering in. They had run over the bridge and climbed the gate, and then they began calling us names and throwing mud. So Hugh John said he would tell on them."

"Didn't," interrupted Hugh John indignantly. "I said I'd knock the heads off them if they didn't stop and get out; and they only laughed and said things about father. So I hit one of them with a stone."

"Then," continued Priscilla, gaining confidence from a certain curious spark of light which began to burn steadily in her father's eyes, "after Hugh John threw the stone, the horrid boys all came and said that they would kill us, and that we had no business there anyway."

"They frowed me down the well, and I went splass! Yes, indeedy!" interrupted Toady Lion, who had imagination.

"Then Donald, our black pet lamb, that is, came into the court, and they all ran away after him and caught him. First he knocked down one or two of them, and then they put a rope round his neck and began to take rides on his back."

"Yes, and he bleated and 'kye-kyed' just feeful!" whimpered Toady Lion, beginning to weep all over again at the remembrance.

But the Smith of the imperial race only clenched his torn hands and looked at his bruised knuckles.

"So Hugh John said he would kill them if they did not let Donald go, and that he was a soldier. But they only laughed louder, and one of them struck him across the lip with a stick—I know him, he's the butch——"

"Shut up, Pris!" shouted Hugh John, with sudden fierceness, "it's dasht-mean to tell names."

"Be quiet, sir," said his father severely; "let your sister finish her story in her own way."

But for all that there was a look of some pride on his face. At that moment Mr. Picton Smith was not sorry to have Hugh John for a son.

"Well," said Priscilla, who had no such scruples as to telling on her enemies, "I won't tell if you say not. But that was the boy who hurt Donald the worst."

"Well, I smashed him for that!" muttered Napoleon Smith.

"And then when Hugh John saw them dragging Donald away and heard him bleating——"

"And 'kye-kying' big, big tears, big as cherries!" interjected Toady Lion, who considered every narrative incomplete to which he did not contribute.

"He was overcome with rage and anger"—at this point Priscilla began to talk by the book, the dignity of the epic tale working on her—"and he rushed upon them fearlessly, though they were ten to one; and they all struck him and kicked him. But Hugh John fought like a lion."

"Yes, like Wichard Toady Lion," cried the namesake of that hero, "and I helpted him and bited a bad boy on the leg, and didn't let go though he kicked and hurted feeful! Yes, indeedy!"

"And I went to their assistance and fought as Hugh John showed me. And—I forget the rest," said Priscilla, her epic style suddenly failing her. Also she felt she must begin to cry very soon, now the strain was over. So she made haste to finish. "But it was dreadful, and they swore, and said they would cut Donald's throat. And one boy took out a great knife and said he knew how to do it. He was the butch——"

"Shut up, Pris! Now don't you dare!" shouted Hugh John, in his most warning tones.

"And when Hugh John rushed in to stop him, he hit him over the head with a stick, and Hugh John fell down. And, oh! I thought he was dead, and I didn't know what to do" (Priscilla was crying in good earnest now); "and I ran to him and tried to lift him up. But I could not—he was so wobbly and soft."

"I bited the boy's leg. It was dood. I bited hard!" interrupted Toady Lion, whose mission had been vengeance.

"And when I looked up again they had taken away p-p-poor Donald," Priscilla went on spasmodically between her tears, "and I think they killed him because he belonged to you, and—they said he had no business there! Oh, they were such horrid cruel boys, and much bigger than us. And I can't bear that Don should have his throat cut. I was promised that he should never be sold for mutton, but only clipped for wool. And he had such a pretty throat to hang daisy-chains on, and was such a dear, dear thing."

"I don't think they would dare to kill him," said Mr. Smith gravely; "besides, they could not lift him over the gate. I will send at once and see. In fact I will go myself!"

There was only anger against the enemy now, and no thought of chastisement of his own in the heart of Mr. Picton Smith. He was rising to reach out his hand to his riding-whip, when General Napoleon Smith, who, like most great makers of history, had taken little part in the telling of it, created a diversion which put all thought of immediate action out of his father's head. He had been standing up, shoulders squared, arms dressed to his side, head erect, as he had seen Sergeant Steel do when he spoke to his Colonel. Once or twice he had swayed slightly, but the heart of the Buonapartes, which beat bravely in his bosom, brought him up again all standing. Nevertheless he grew even whiter and whiter, till, all in a moment, he gave a little lurch forward, checked himself, and again looked straight before him. Then he sobbed out once suddenly and helplessly, said "I couldn't help getting beaten, father—there were too many of them!" and fell over all of a piece on the hearthrug.

At which his father's face grew very still and angry as he gathered the great General gently in his arms and carried him upstairs to his own little white cot.

CHAPTER VII

THE POOR WOUNDED HUSSAR.

IT is small wonder that Mr. Picton Smith was full of anger. His castle had been invaded and desecrated, his authority as proprietor defied, his children insulted and abused. As a magistrate he felt bound to take notice both of the outrage and of the theft of his property. As a father he could not easily forget the plight in which his three children had appeared before him.

But in his schemes of vengeance he reckoned without that distinguished military officer, General-Field-Marshal Napoleon Smith. For this soldier had been promoted on his bed of sickness. He had read somewhere that in his profession (as in most others) success quite often bred envy and neglect, but that to the unsuccessful, promotion and honour were sometimes awarded as a sort of consolation sweepstakes. So, having been entirely routed and plundered by the enemy, it came to Hugh John in the watches of the night—when, as he put it, "his head was hurting like fun" that it was time for him to take the final step in his own advancement.

So on the next morning he announced the change in his name and style to his army as it filed in to visit him. The army was on the whole quite agreeable.

"But I'm afraid I shall never remember all that, Mr. General-Field-Marshal Napoleon Smith!" said Priscilla.

"Well, you'd better!" returned the wounded hero, as truculently as he could for the bandages and the sticking-plaster, in which he was swathed after the fashion of an Egyptian mummy partially unwrapped.

"What a funny smell!" piped Toady Lion. "Do field-marshals all smell like that?"

"Get out, silly!" retorted the wounded officer. "Don't you know that's the stuff they rub on the wounded when they have fought bravely? That's arnicay!"

"And what do they yub on them when they don't fight bravely?" persisted Toady Lion, who had had enough of fighting, and who in his heart was resolved that the next time he would "yun away" as hard as he could, a state of mind not unusual after the zip-zip of bullets is heard for the first time.

"First of all they catch them and kick them for being cowards. Then they shoot at them till they are dead; and may the Lord have mercy on their souls! Amen!" said General Smith, mixing things for the information and encouragement of Sir Toady Lion.

Presently the children were called out to go and play, and the wounded hero was left alone. His head ached so that he could not read. Indeed, in any case he could not, for the room was darkened with the intention of shielding his damaged eyes from the light. General Napoleon could only watch the flies buzzing round and round, and wish in vain that he had a fly-flapper at the end of a pole in order to "plop" them, as he used to do all over the house in the happy days before Janet Sheepshanks discovered what made the walls and windows so horrid with dead and dying insects.

"Yes; the squashy ones were rather streaky!" had been the words in which Hugh John admitted his guilt, after the pole and leathern flapper were taken from him and burned in the washhouse fire.

Thus in the semi-darkness Hugh John lay watching the flies with the stealthy intentness of a Red Indian scalper on the trail. It was sad to lie idly in bed, so bewrapped and swathed that (as he mournfully remarked), "if one of the brutes were to settle on your nose, you could only wait for him to crawl up, and then snatch at him with your left eyelid."

Suddenly the disabled hero bethought himself of something. First, after listening intently so as to be quite sure that "the children" were outside the bounds of the house, the wounded general raised himself on his elbow. But the effort hurt him so much that involuntarily he said "Outch!" and sank back again on the pillow.

"Crikey, but don't I smell just!" he muttered, when, after one breath of purer air, he sank back into the pool of arnica vapour. "I suppose I'll have to howl out for Janet. What a swot!"

"Janet!—Ja-a-a-a-net!" he shouted, and sighed a sigh of relief to find that at least there was one part of him neither bandaged nor drowned in arnica.

"Deil tak' the laddie!" cried Janet, who went about her work all day with one ear cocked toward the chamber of her brave sick soldier; "what service is there in taking the rigging aff the hoose wi' your noise? Did ye think I was doon at Edam Cross? What do ye want, callant, that ye deafen my auld lugs like that? I never heard sic a laddie!"

But General Smith did not answer any of these questions. He well knew Janet's tone of simulated anger when she was "putting it on."

"Go and fetch it!" he said darkly.

CHAPTER VIII

THE FAMILIAR SPIRIT.

NOW there was a skeleton in the cupboard of General Napoleon Smith. No distinguished family can be respectable without at least one such. But that of the new field-marshal was particularly dark and disgraceful.

Very obediently Janet Sheepshanks vanished from the sick-room, and presently returned with an oblong parcel, which she handed to the hero of battles.

"Thank you," he said; "are you sure that the children are out?"

"They are sailing paper boats on the mill-dam," said Janet, going to the window to look.

Hugh John sighed a sigh. He wished he could sail boats on the mill-dam.

"I hope every boat will go down the mill lade, and get mashed in the wheel," he said pleasantly.

"For shame, Master Hugh!" replied Janet Sheepshanks, shaking her head at him, but conscious that he was exactly expressing her own mind, if she had been lying sick a-bed and had been compelled to listen to some other housekeeper jingling keys that once were hers, ransacking her sacredest repositories, and keeping in order the menials of the house.

Hugh John proceeded cautiously to unwrap his family skeleton. Presently from the folds of tissue paper a very aged and battered "Sambo" emerged. Now a "Sambo" is a black woolly-haired negro doll of the fashion of many years ago. This specimen was dressed in simple and airy fashion in a single red shell jacket. As to the rest, he was bare and black from head to foot. Janet called him "that horrid object"; but, nevertheless, he was precious in the eyes of Hugh John, and therefore in hers.

Though twelve years of age, he still liked to carry on dark and covert intercourse with his ancient "Sambo." In public, indeed, he preached, in season and out of season, against the folly and wickedness of dolls. No one but a lassie or a "lassie-boy" would do such a thing. He laughed at Priscilla for cleaning up her doll's kitchen once a week, and for organising afternoon tea-parties for her quiet harem. But secretly he would have liked very well to see Sambo sit at that bounteous board.

Nevertheless, he instructed Toady Lion every day with doctrine and reproof that it was "only for girls" to have dolls. And knowing well that none of his common repositories were so remote and sacred as long to escape Priscilla's unsleeping eye, or the more stormy though fitful curiosity of Sir Toady Lion, Hugh John had been compelled to take his ancient nurse and ever faithful friend Janet into his confidence. So Sambo dwelt in the housekeeper's pantry and had two distinct odours. One side of him smelt of paraffin, and the other of soft soap, which, to a skilled detective, might have revealed the secret of his dark abode.

But let us not do our hero an injustice.

It was not exactly as a doll that General Smith considered Sambo. By no means so, indeed. Sometimes he was a distinguished general who came to take orders from his chief, sometimes an awkward private who needed to be drilled, and then knocked spinning across the floor for inattention to orders. For, be it remembered, it was the custom in the army of Field-Marshal-General Smith for the Commander-in-Chief to drill the recruits with his own voice, and in the by no means improbable event of their proving stupid, to knock them endwise with his own august hand.

But it was as Familiar Spirit, and in the pursuit of occult divination, that General Napoleon most frequently resorted to Sambo. He had read all he could find in legend and history concerning that gruesomely attractive goblin, clothed all in red, which the wicked Lord Soulis kept in an oaken chest in a castle not so far from his own father's house of Windy Standard.

And Hugh John saw no reason why Sambo should not be the very one. Spirits do not die. It is a known fact that they are fond of their former haunts. What, then, could be clearer? Sambo was evidently Lord Soulis' Red Imp risen from the dead. Was Sambo not black? The devil was black. Did Sambo not wear a red coat? Was not the demon of the oaken chest attired in flaming scarlet, when all cautiously he lifted the lid at midnight and looked wickedly out upon his master?

Yet the General was conscious that Sambo Soulis was a distinct disappointment in the part of familiar spirit. He would sit silent, with his head hanging idiotically on one side, when he was asked to reveal the deepest secrets of the future, instead of toeing the line and doing it. Nor was it recorded in the chronicles of Soulis that the original demon of the chest had had his nose "bashed flat" by his master, as Hugh John vigorously expressed the damaged appearance of his own familiar.

Worse than all, Hugh John had tried to keep Sambo in his rabbit-box. But not only did he utterly fail to put his "fearful head, crowned with a red night-cap" over the edge of the hutch at the proper time—as, had he been of respectable parentage, he would not have failed to do, but, in addition, he developed in his close quarters an animal odour so pungent and unprofitable that Janet Sheepshanks refused to admit him into the store-cupboard till he had been thoroughly fumigated and disinfected. So for a whole week Sambo Soulis swung ignominiously by the neck from the clothes line, and Hugh John went about in fear of the questioning of the children or of the confiscation by his father of his well-beloved but somewhat unsatisfactory familiar spirit.

It was in order to consult him on a critical point of doctrine and practice that Hugh John had now sent for Sambo Soulis.

He propped him up before him against a pillow, on which he sat bent forward at an acute angle from the hips, as if ready to pounce upon his master and rend him to pieces so soon as the catechism should be over.

"Look here," said General-Field-Marshal Smith to the oracle, "supposing the governor tells me to split on Nipper Donnan, the butcher boy, will it be dasht-mean if I do?"

Sambo Soulis, being disturbed by the delicacy of the question or perhaps by the wriggling of Hugh John upon his pillow, only lurched drivellingly forward.

"Sit up and answer," cried his master, "or else I'll hike you out of that pretty quick, for a silly old owl!"

And with his least bandaged hand he gave Sambo a sound cuff on the side of his venerable battered head, before propping him up at a new angle with his chin on his knees.

"Now speak up, Soulis," said General Smith; "I ask you would it be dasht-mean?"

The oracle was understood to joggle his chin and goggle his eyes. He certainly did the latter.

"I thought so," said Soulis' master, as is usual in such cases, interpreting the reply oracular according to his liking. "But look here, how are we to get back Donald unless we split? Would it not be all right to split just to get Donald back?"

Sambo Soulis waggled his head again. This time his master looked a little more serious.

"I suppose you are right," he said pensively, "but if it would be dasht-mean to split, we must just try to get him back ourselves—that is, if the beasts have not cut his throat, as they said they would."

CHAPTER IX

PUT TO THE QUESTION.

IN the chaste retirement of his sick room the Field-Marshal had just reached this conclusion, when he heard a noise in the hall. There was a sound of the gruff unmirthful voices of grown-ups, a scuffling of feet, a planting of whips and walking-sticks on the zinc-bottomed hall-stand, and then, after a pause which meant drinks, heavy footsteps in the passage which led to the hero's chamber.

Hugh John snatched up Sambo Soulis and thrust him deep beneath the bedclothes, where he could readily push him over the end with his toes, if it should chance to be "the doctor-beast" come to uncover him and "fool with the bandages." I have said enough to show that the General was not only frankly savage in sentiment, but resembled his great imperial namesake in being grateful only when it suited him.

Before General Napoleon had his toes fairly settled over the back of Sambo Soulis' neck, so as to be able to remove him out of harm's way on any sudden alarm, the door opened and his father came in, ushering two men, the first of whom came forward to the bedside in an easy, kindly manner, and held out his hand.

"Do you know me?" he said, giving Hugh John's second sorest hand such a squeeze that the wounded hero was glad it was not the very sorest one.

"Yes," replied the hero promptly, "you are Sammy Carter's father. I can jolly well lick——"

"Hugh John," interrupted his father severely, "remember what you are saying to Mr. Davenant Carter."

"Well, anyway, I can lick Sammy Carter till he's dumb-sick!" muttered the General between his teeth, as he avoided the three pairs of eyes that were turned upon him.

"Oh, let him say just what he likes!" said Mr. Davenant Carter jovially. "Sammy is the better of being licked, if that is what the boy was going to say. I sometimes try my hand at it myself with some success."

The other man who had come in with Mr. Smith was a thick-set fellow of middle height, with a curious air of being dressed up in somebody else's clothes. Yet they fitted him very well. He wore on his face (in addition to a slight moustache) an expression which somehow made Hugh John think guiltily of all the orchards he had ever visited along with Toady Lion and Sammy Carter's sister Cissy, who was "no end of a nice girl" in Hugh John's estimation.

"This, Hugh," said his father, with a little wave of his hand, "is Mr. Mant, the Chief Constable of the county. Mr. Carter and he have come to ask you a few questions, which you will answer at once."

"I won't be dasht-mean!" muttered Napoleon Smith to himself.

"What's that?" ejaculated Mr. Smith, catching the echo of his son's rumble of dissent.

"Only my leg that hurted," said the hypocritical hero of battles.

"Don't you think we should have the other children here?" said Mr. Chief Constable Mant, speaking for the first time in a gruff, move-on-there voice.

"Certainly," assented Mr. Smith, going to the door. "Janet!"

"Yes, sir!"

The answer came from immediately behind the door.

The Field-Marshal's brow darkened, or rather it would have done so if there had been no white bandages over it. This is the correct expression anyhow—though ordinary brows but seldom behave in this manner.

"Prissy's all right," he thought to himself, "but if that little fool Toady Lion——"

And he clenched his second sorest hand under the clothes, and kicked Sambo Soulis to the foot of the bed in a way which augured but little mercy to Sir Toady Lion if, after all his training, he should turn out "dasht-mean" in the hour of trial.

Presently the other two children were pushed in at the door, Toady Lion trying a bolt at the last moment, which Janet Sheepshanks easily foiled by catching at the slack of his trousers behind, while Prissy stood holding her hands primly as if in Sunday-school class. Both afforded to the critical eye of Hugh John complete evidence that they had only just escaped from the Greater Pain of the comb and soaped flannel-cloth of Janet Sheepshanks. Prissy's curls were still wet and smoothed out, and Toady Lion was trying in vain to rub the yellow soap out of his eyes.

So at the headquarters of its general, the army of Windy Standard formed up. Sir Toady Lion wished to get within supporting distance of Prissy, and accordingly kept snuggling nearer all the time, so that he could get a furtive hold of her skirts at awkward places in the examination. This he could do the more easily that General Field-Marshal Smith was prevented by the bandages over his right eye, and also by the projecting edges of the pillow, from seeing Toady Lion's left hand.

"Now, Priscilla," began her father, "tell Mr. Davenant Carter and Mr. Mant what happened in the castle, and the names of any of the bad boys who stole your pet lamb."

"Wasn't no lamb—Donald was a sheep, and he could fight," began Toady Lion, without relevance, but with his usual eagerness to hear the sound of his own piping voice. In his zeal he took a step forward and so brought himself on the level of the eye of his general, who from the pillow darted upon him a look so freezing that Sir Toady Lion instantly fell back into the ranks, and clutched Prissy's skirt with such energy as almost to stagger her severe deportment.

"Now," said the Chief Constable of Bordershire, "tell me what were the names of the assailants."

He was listening to the tale as told by Prissy with his note-book ready in his hand, occasionally biting at the butt of the pencil, and anon wetting the lead in his mouth, under the mistaken idea that by so doing he improved its writing qualities.

"I think," began Prissy, "that they were——"

"A-chew!" came from the bed and from under the bandages with a sudden burst of sound. Field-Marshal Napoleon Smith had sneezed. That was all.

But Prissy started. She knew what it meant. It was the well-known signal not to commit herself under examination.

Her father looked round at the open windows.

"Are you catching cold with the draught, Hugh John?" he asked kindly.

"I think I have a little cold," said the wily General, who did not wish all the windows to be promptly shut.

"Don't know all their names, but the one that hurted me was——" began Toady Lion.

But who the villain was will never be known, for at that moment the bedclothes became violently disturbed immediately in front of Sir Toady Lion's nose. A fearful black countenance nodded once at him and disappeared.

"Black Sambo!" gasped Toady Lion, awed by the terrible appearance, and falling back from the place where the wizard had so suddenly appeared.

"What did I understand you to say, little boy?" said Mr. Mant, with his pencil on his book.

"Ow—it was Black Sambo!" Toady Lion almost screamed. Mr. Mant gravely noted the fact.

"What in the world does he mean?" asked Mr. Mant, casting his eyes searchingly from Prissy to General Napoleon and back again.

"He means 'Black Sambo'!" said Prissy, devoting herself strictly to facts, and leaving the Chief Constable to his proper business of interpreting them.

"What is his other name?" said Mr. Mant.

"Soulis!" said General Smith from the bed.

The three gentlemen looked at each other, smiled, and shook their heads.

"What did I tell you?" said Mr. Davenant Carter. "Try as I will, I cannot get the simplest thing out of my Sammy and Cissy if they don't choose to tell."

Nevertheless Mr. Smith, being a sanguine man and with little experience of children, tried again.

"There is no black boy in the neighbourhood," said Mr. Smith severely; "now tell the truth, children—at once, when I bid you!"

He uttered the last words in a loud and commanding tone.

"Us is telling the troof, father dear," said Toady Lion, in the "coaxy-woaxy" voice which he used when he wanted marmalade from Janet or a ride on the saddle from Mr. Picton Smith.

"Perhaps the boy had blackened his face to deceive the eye," suggested Mr. Mant, with the air of one familiar from infancy with the tricks and devices of the evil-minded of all ages.

"Was the ringleader's face blackened?—Answer at once!" said Mr. Smith sternly.

The General extracted his bruised and battered right hand from under the clothes and looked at it.

"I think so," he said, "leastways some has come off on my knuckles!"

Mr. Davenant Carter burst into a peal of jovial mirth.

"Didn't I tell you?—It isn't a bit of use badgering children when they don't want to tell. Let's go over to the castle."

And with that the three gentlemen went out, while Napoleon Smith, Prissy, and Sir Toady Lion were left alone.

The General beckoned them to his bedside with his nose—quite an easy thing to do if you have the right kind of nose, which Hugh John had.

"Now look here," he said, "if you'd told, I'd have jolly well flattened you when I got up. 'Tisn't our business to tell p'leecemen things."

"That wasn't a p'leeceman," said Sir Toady Lion, "hadn't no shiny buttons."

"That's the worst kind," said the General in a low, hissing whisper; "all the same you stood to it like bricks, and now I'm going to get well and begin on the campaign at once."

"Don't you be greedy-teeth and eat it all yourself!" interjected Toady Lion, who thought that the campaign was something to eat, and that it sounded good.

"What are you going to do?" said Prissy, who had a great belief in the executive ability of her brother.

"I know their secret hold," said General-Field-Marshal Smith grandly, "and in the hour of their fancied security we will fall upon them and——"

"And what?" gasped Prissy and Toady Lion together, awaiting the revelation of the horror.

"Destroy them!" said General Smith, in a tone which was felt by all parties to be final.

He laid himself back on his pillow and motioned them haughtily away. Prissy and Sir Toady Lion retreated on tiptoe, lest Janet should catch them and send them to the parlour—Prissy to read her chapter, and her brother along with her to keep him out of mischief.

And so the great soldier was left to his meditations in the darkened hospital chamber.

CHAPTER X

A SCOUTING ADVENTURE.

GENERAL SMITH, having now partially recovered, was mustering his forces and arranging his plans of campaign. He had spoken no hasty word when he boasted that he knew the secret haunt of the robbers. For, some time before, during a brief but glorious career as a pirate, he had been brought into connection with Nipper Donnan, the strongest butcher's boy of the town, and the ringleader in all mischief, together with Joe Craig, Nosie Cuthbertson, and Billy M'Robert, his ready followers.

Hugh John had once been a member of the Comanche Cowboys, as Nipper Donnan's band was styled; but a disagreement about the objects of attack had hastened a rupture, and the affair of the castle was but the last act in a hostility long latent. In fact the war was always simmering, and was ready to boil over on the slightest provocation. For when Hugh John found that his father's orchards, his father's covers and hencoops were to be the chief prey (being safer than the farmers' yards, where there were big dogs always loose, and the town streets, where "bobbies" mostly congregated), he struck. He reflected that one day all these things would belong to himself. He would share with Prissy and Sir Toady Lion, of course; but still mainly they would belong to him. Why then plunder them now? The argument was utilitarian but sufficient.

Though he did not mention the fact to Prissy or Sir Toady Lion, Hugh John was perfectly well acquainted with the leaders in the fray at the castle. He knew also that there were motives for the enmity of the Comanche Cowboys other and deeper than the town rights to the possession of the Castle of Windy Standard.

It was night when Hugh John cautiously pushed up the sash of his window and looked out. A few stars were high up aloft wandering through the grey-blue fields of the summer night, as it were listlessly and with their hands in their pockets. A corn-crake cried in the meadow down below, steadily, remorselessly, like the aching of a tooth. A white owl passed the window with an almost noiseless whiff of fluffy feathers. Hugh John sniffed the cool pungent night smell of the dew on the near wet leaves and the distant mown grass. It always went to his head a little, and was the only thing which made him regret that he was to be a soldier. Whenever he smelt it, he wanted to be an explorer of far-off lands, or an honest poacher—even a gamekeeper might do, in case the other vocations proved unattainable.

Hugh John got out of the window slowly, leaving Sir Toady Lion asleep and the door into Prissy's room wide open. He dropped easily and lightly upon the roof of the wash-house, and, steadying himself upon the tiles, he slid down till he heard Cæsar, the black Newfoundland, stir in his kennel. Then he called him softly, so that he might not bark. He could not take him with him to-night, for though Cæsar was little more than a puppy his step was like that of a cow, and when released he went blundering end on through the woods like a festive avalanche. Hugh John's father, for reasons of his own, persisted in calling him "The Potwalloping Elephant."

So, having assured himself that Cæsar would not bark, the boy dropped to the ground, taking the roof of the dog-kennel on the way. Cæsar stirred, rolled himself round, and came out breathing hard, and thump-thumping Hugh John's legs with his thick tail, with distinctly audible blows.

Then when he understood that he was not to be taken, he sat down at the extremity of his chain and regarded his master wistfully through the gloom with his head upon one side; and as Hugh John took his way down the avenue, Cæsar moaned a little, intoning his sense of injury and disappointment as the parson does a litany.

At the first turn of the road Hugh John had just time to dart aside into the green, acrid-scented, leathery-leaved shrubbery, where he lay crouched with his hands on his knees and his head thrust forward, while Tom the keeper went slowly by with his arm about Jane Housemaid's waist.

"WAIT TILL THE NEXT TIME YOU WON'T LEND ME THE FERRET, TOM CANNON! O-HO, JANE HOUSEMAID, WILL YOU TELL MY FATHER THE NEXT TIME I TAKE YOUR DUST SCOOP?"

"Aha!" chuckled Hugh John; "wait till the next time you won't lend me the ferret, Tom Cannon! O-ho, Jane Housemaid, will you tell my father the next time I take your dust scoop out to the sand-hole to help dig trenches? I think not!"

And Hugh John hugged himself in his pleasure at having a new weapon so admirably double-barrelled. He looked upon the follies of love, as manifested in the servants' hall and upon the outskirts of the village, as so much excellent material by which a wise man would not fail to profit. Janet Sheepshanks was very severe on such delinquencies, and his father—well, Hugh John felt that Tom Cannon would not wish to appear before his master in such a connection. He had a vague remembrance of a certain look he had once seen on his father's face when Allan Chestney, the head-keeper, came out from Mr. Picton Smith's workroom with these words ringing in his ear, "Now, sir, you will do as I tell you, or I will give you a character—but, such a character as you will carry through the world with you, and which will be buried with you when you die."

Allan was now married to Jemima, who had once been cook at the house of Windy Standard. Hugh John went over to their cottage often to eat her delicious cakes; and when Allan came in from the woods, his wife ordered him to take off his dirty boots before he entered her clean kitchen. Then Allan Chestney would re-enter and play submissively and furtively with Patty Pans, their two-year-old child, shifting his chair obediently whenever Cook Jemima told him. But all the same, Hugh John felt dimly that these things would not have happened, save for the look on his father's face when Allan Chestney went in to see him that day in the grim pine-boarded workroom.

So, much lightened in his mind by his discovery, Hugh John took his way down the avenue. At the foot of it, and before he came to the locked white gate and the cottage of Betty, he turned aside through a copse, over a little green patch of sward on which his feet slid smooth as velvet. A hare sat on the edge of this, with her fore-feet in the air. She was for the moment so astonished at Hugh John's appearance that it was an appreciable period of time before she turned, and with a quick, sidelong rush disappeared into the wood. He could hear the soughing rush of the river below him, which took different keys according to the thickness of the tree copses which were folded about it; now singing gaily through the thin birches and rowans; anon humming more hoarsely through the alders; again rustling and whispering mysteriously through the grey shivery poplars; and, last of all, coming up, dull and sullen, through the heavy oak woods, whose broad leaves cover all noises underneath them as a blanket muffles speech.

Hugh John skirted the river till he came to the stepping-stones, which he crossed with easy confidence. He knew them—high, low, Jack, and game, like the roofs of his father's outhouses. He could just as easily have gone across blindfold.

Then he made his way over the wide, yellowish-grey spaces of the castle island, avoiding the copses of willow and dwarf birch, and the sandy-bottomed "bunkers," which ever and anon gleamed up before him like big tawny eyes out of the dusky grey-green of the short grass. After a little the walls of the old castle rose grimly before him, and he could hear the starlings scolding one another sleepily high up in the crevices. A black-cap piped wistfully among the sedges of the watermarsh. Hugh John had often heard that the ruin was haunted, and certainly he always held his breath as he passed it. But now he was on duty, and, if need had been, he would that night have descended to the deepest dungeon, and faced a full Banquo-board of blood-boltered ghosts.

CHAPTER XI

ENEMY'S COUNTRY.

HE presently came to the wooden bridge and crossed it. He was now on the outskirts of the town, and in enemy's country. So, more from etiquette than precaution, he took the shelter of a wall, glided through a plantation, among the withy roots of which his foot presently caught in a brass "grin," or rabbit's snare. Hugh John grubbed it up gratefully and pocketed it. He had no objections whatever to spoiling the Egyptians.

He was now in butcher Donnan's pastures, where many fore-doomed sheep, in all the bliss of ignorance, waited their turns to be made into mutton. Very anxiously Hugh John scrutinised each one. He wandered round and round till he had made certain that Donald was not there.

At the foot of the pasture were certain black-pitched wooden sheds set in a square, with a little yard like a church pew in the midst. Somewhere here, he knew, slept Donnan's slaughterman, and it was possible that in this place Donald might be held in captivity.

Now it was an accomplishment of our hero's that he could bleat like any kind of sheep—except perhaps an old tup, for which his voice was as yet too shrill. In happy, idle days he had elaborated a code of signals with Donald, and was well accustomed to communicating with him from his bedroom window. So now he crouched in the dusk of the hedge, and said "Maa-aaa!" in a tone of reproach.

Instantly a little answering bleat came from the black sheds, a sound which made Hugh's heart beat faster. Still he could not be quite sure. He therefore bleated again more pleadingly, and again there came back the answer, choked and feeble indeed, but quite obviously the voice of his own dear Donald. Hugh John cast prudence to the winds. He raced round and climbed the bars into the enclosure, calling loudly, "Donald! Donald!"

But hardly had his feet touched the ground when a couple of dogs flew at him from the corner of the yard, and he had scarcely time to get on the top of a stone wall before they were clamouring and yelping beneath him. Hugh John crouched on his "hunkers" (as he called the posture in which one sits on a wall when hostile dogs are leaping below), and seizing a large coping-stone he dropped it as heavily as he could on the head of the nearer and more dangerous. A howl most lamentable immediately followed. Then a man's voice cried, "Down, Towser! What's the matter, Grip? Sic' them! Good dogs!"

It was the voice of the slaughterman, roused from his slumbers, and in fear of tramps or other midnight marauders upon his master's premises.

Hugh ran on all fours along the wall to the nearest point of the woods, dropped over, and with a leaping, anxious heart sped in the direction of home. He crossed the bridge in safety, but as he ran across the island he could hear the dogs upon the trail and the encouraging shouts of his pursuer. The black looming castle fell swiftly behind him. Now he was at the stepping-stones, over which he seemed to float rather than leap, so completely had fear added to his usual strength wings of swiftness.

But at the farther side the dogs were close upon him. He was obliged to climb a certain low tree, where he had often sat dangling his legs and swinging in the branches while he allowed Prissy to read to him.

The dogs were soon underneath, and he could see them leaping upward with snapping white teeth which gleamed unpleasantly through the darkness. But their furious barking was promptly answered. Hugh John could hear a heavy tread approaching among the dense foliage of the trees. A dark form suddenly appeared in the glade and poised something at its shoulder.—Flash! There came a deafening report, the thresh of leaden drops, a howl of pain from the dogs, and both of them took their way back towards the town with not a few bird shot in their flanks.

Hugh John's heart stood still as the dark figure advanced. He feared it might prove to be his father. Instead it was Tom Cannon, and the brave scout on the tree heaved a sigh of relief.

"Who's up there?" cried the under-keeper gruffly; "come down this moment and show yourself, you dirty poacher, or by Heaven I'll shoot you sitting!"

"All right, Tom, I'm coming as fast as I can," said Hugh John, beginning to clamber down.

"Heavens and earth, Master Hugh—what be you doing here? Whatever will master say?"

"He won't say anything, for he won't know, Tom Cannon." said Hugh John confidently.

"Oh yes, he will," said the keeper. "I won't have you bringing a pack of dogs into my covers at twelve of the clock—blow me if I will!"

"Well, you won't tell my father, anyway!" said Hugh John calmly, dusting himself as well as he could.

"And why not?" asked the keeper indignantly.

"'Cause if you do, I'll tell where I saw you kissing Jane Housemaid an hour ago!"

Now this was at once a guess and an exaggeration. Hugh John had not seen all this, but he felt rather than knew that the permitted arm about Jane Housemaid's waist could have no other culmination. Also he had a vague sense that this was the most irritating thing he could say in the circumstances.

At any rate Tom Cannon fairly gasped with astonishment. A double-jointed word slipped between his teeth, which sounded like "Hang that boy!" At last his seething thoughts found utterance.

"You young imp of Satan—it ain't true, anyway."

"All right, you can tell my father that!" said Hugh John coolly, feeling the strength of his position.

Tom Cannon was not much frightened for himself, but he did not wish to get Jane Housemaid into any trouble, for, as he well knew, that young woman had omitted to ask for leave of absence. So he only said, "All right, it's none of my business if you wander over every acre, and break your neck off every tree on the blame estate. But you'd better be getting home before master comes out and catches you himself! Then you'd eat strap, my lad!"

So having remade the peace, Tom escorted Hugh John back to the dog kennel with great good nature, and even gave him a leg up to the roof above the palace of Cæsar.

Hugh John paused as he put one foot into the bedroom, heavy and yet homelike with the night smell of a sleeping house. Toady Lion had fallen out of bed and lay, still with his blanket wrapped round him like a martial cloak, half under his cot and half on the floor. But this he did every other night. Prissy was breathing quietly in the next room. All was safe.

Hugh John called softly down, "Tom, Tom!"

"What now?" returned the keeper, who had been spying along the top windows to distinguish a certain one dear to his heart.

"I say, Tom—I'll tell Jane Housemaid to-morrow that you're a proper brick."

"Thank'ee, sir!" said Tom, saluting gravely and turning off across the lawn towards the "bothy," where among the pine woods he kept his owl-haunted bachelor quarters.

CHAPTER XII

MOBILISATION.

GENERALLY speaking, Hugh John despised Sammy Carter—first, because he could lick him with one hand, and, secondly, because Sammy Carter was a clever boy and could discover ways of getting even without licking him. Clever boys are all cheeky and need hammering. Besides, Sammy Carter was in love with Prissy, and every one knew what that meant. But then Sammy Carter had a sister, Cissy by name, and she was quite a different row of beans.

Furthermore, Sammy Carter read books—a degrading pursuit, unless they had to do with soldiering, and especially with the wars of Napoleon, Hugh John's great ancestor. In addition, Sammy knew every date that was, and would put you right in a minute if you said that Bannockburn happened after Waterloo, or any little thing like that. A disposition so perverse as this could only be cured with a wicket or with Hugh John's foot, and our hero frequently applied both corrections.

But Cissy Carter—ah! now there was a girl if you like. She never troubled about such things. She could not run so fast as Prissy, but then she had a perfect colt's mane of hair, black and glossy, which flew out behind her when she did. Moreover, she habitually did what Hugh John told her, and burned much incense at his shrine, so that modest youth approved of her. It was of her he first thought when he set about organising his army for the assault upon the Black Sheds, where, like Hofer at Mantua, the gallant Donald lay in chains.

But it was written in the chronicles of Oaklands that Cissy Carter could not be allowed over the river without Sammy, so Sammy would have to be permitted to join too. Hugh John resolved that he would keep his eye very sharply upon Prissy and Sammy Carter, for the abandoned pair had been known to compose poetry in the heat of an engagement, and even to read their compositions to one another on the sly. For this misdemeanour Prissy would certainly have been court-martialled, only that her superior officer could not catch her at the time. But the wicked did not wholly escape, for Hugh John tugged her hair afterwards till she cried; whereat Janet Sheepshanks, coming suddenly upon him and cornering him, spanked him till he cried. He cried solely as a measure of military necessity, because it was the readiest way of getting Janet to stop, and also because that day Janet wore a new pair of slippers, with heels upon which Hugh John had not been counting. So he cried till he got out of Janet's reach, when he put out his tongue at her and said, "Hum-m! Thought you hurt, didn't you? Well, it just didn't a bit!"

And Sir Toady Lion, who was feeding his second-best wooden horses with wild sand-oats gathered green, remarked, "When I have childwens I sail beat them wif a big boot and tackets in the heel."

Which voiced with great precision Janet Sheepshanks' mood at that moment.

The army of Windy Standard, then, when fully mustered, consisted of General-Field-Marshal Napoleon Smith, Commander-in-Chief and regimental Sergeant-Major (also, on occasions of parade, Big Big-Drummer); Adjutant-General Cissy Carter, promoted to her present high position for always agreeing with her superior officer—a safe rule in military politics;

Commissariat-Sergeant Sir Toady Lion, who declined any other post than the care of the provisions, and had to be conciliated; together with Privates Sammy Carter and Prissy Smith. Sammy Carter had formerly been Adjutant, because he had a pony, but gallantly resigned in order to be of the same rank as Prissy, who was the sole member of the force wholly without military ambition.

At the imposing review which was held on the plains of Windy Standard, the Commander-in-Chief insisted on carrying the blue banner himself, as well as the big-big drum, till Sammy Carter, who had not yet resigned, offered him his pony to ride upon. This he did with guile and malice aforethought, for on the drum being elevated in front of the mounted officer, Polo promptly ran away, and deposited General-Field-Marshal Smith in the horse pond.

"DEPOSITED GENERAL-FIELD-MARSHAL SMITH IN THE HORSE POND."

But this force, though officered with consummate ability, was manifestly insufficient for the attack upon the Black Sheds. This was well shown by Sammy Carter, who also pointed out that the armies of all ages had never been exclusively composed of those of noble birth. There were, for example, at Bannockburn, the knights, the esquires, the sturdy yeomanry, the spearmen, the bowmen, and the camp-followers. He advised that the stable boys, Mike and Peter, should be approached.

Now the head stable boy, Mike O'Donelly by name, was a scion of the noblest Bourbon race. His father was an exile, who spoke the language with a strong foreign accent, and drove a fish cart—which also had a pronounced accent, reputed deadly up to fifty yards with a favourable wind.

"Foine frish hirrings—foive for sixpince!" was the way he said it. This proved to demonstration that he came from a far land, and was the descendant of kings. When taxed directly with being the heir to a crown, he did not deny it, but said, "Yus, Masther Smith, wanst I had a crown, but I lost it. 'Twas the Red Lion, bad scran to ut, that did the deed!"

Now this was evidently only a picturesque and regal way of referring to the bloody revolution by which King Michael O'Donowitch had been dethroned and reduced to driving a fish-cart—the old, old story, doubtless, of royal license and popular ingratitude. But there was no such romantic mystery about Peter Greg. He was simply junior stable boy, and his father was general utility man—or, as it was more generally called, "odd man," about the estate of Windy Standard. Peter occupied most of his time in keeping one eye on his work and the other on his father, who, on general utility principles, "welted" him every time that he caught him. This exercise, and his other occupation of perpetual fisticuffs with Prince Mike O'Donelly, had so developed his muscles and trained his mind, that he could lick any other two boys of his size in the parish. He said so himself, and he usually had at least one black eye to show for it. So no one contradicted him, and, indeed, who had a better right to know?

Prince Michael O'Donowitch (the improvement in style was Sammy Carter's) put the matter differently. He said, "I can lick Peter Greg till he can't stand" ("shtand" was how the royal exile pronounced it), "but Peter an' me can knock the stuffin' out of any half-dozen spalpeens in this dirthy counthry."

Both Mike and Peter received commissions in the army at the same moment. The ceremony took place at the foot of the great hay mow at the back of the stable yard. In view of his noble ancestry, Prince Michael O'Donowitch was made a major-general, and Peter a lieutenant of marines. The newly appointed officers instantly clinched, fell headlong, rolled over and over one another, pommelled each other's heads, bit, scratched, and kicked till the hay and straw flew in all directions.

When the dust finally cleared away, Peter was found sitting astride of Prince Michael, and shouting, "Are you the general-major, or am I?"

Then when they had risen to their feet and dusted themselves, it was found that the distinguished officers had exchanged commissions, and that Peter Greg had become major-general, while Prince Michael O'Donowitch was lieutenant of marines, with a new and promising black eye!

"GENERALS OF DIVISION, EQUAL IN RANK."

But at the first drill, upon General Peter issuing some complicated order, such as "Attention! eyes right!" Lieutenant O'Donowitch remarked, "Me eyes is as roight as yours, ye dirthy baste av a Scotchy!" Whereupon, as the result of another appeal to arms, the former judgment was reversed, and Prince Michael regained his commission at the price of another black eye. Indeed he would have had three, but for the fact that the number of his eyes was somewhat strictly limited to two.

Now it was felt by all parties that in a well-disciplined army such transitions were altogether too sudden, and so a compromise was suggested—as usual by Sammy Carter. Prince Michael and Peter Greg were both made generals of division, equal in rank, under Field-Marshal Smith. The division commanded by General Peter was composed of Cissy and Sir Toady Lion. The command of this first division proved, however, to be purely nominal, for Cissy was much too intimate with the Commander-in-Chief to be ordered about, and as for Toady Lion he was so high minded and irresponsible that he quite declined to obey anybody whatsoever. Still, the title was the thing, and "the division of General Peter Greg" sounded very well.

The other division was much more subordinate. Prissy and Sammy Carter were the only genuine privates, and they were quite ready to be commanded by General Mike, Prissy upon conscientious non-resistance principles, and Sammy with a somewhat humorous aside to his fellow-soldier that it wouldn't be very bad, because Mike's father (the royal fish-hawker) lived on Sammy's ancestral domain, and owed money to Mr. Davenant Carter.

Thus even the iron discipline of a British army is tempered to the sacred property holder.

The immediate advance of the army of Windy Standard upon the Black Sheds was only hindered by a somewhat serious indisposition which suddenly attacked the Commander-in-Chief. The facts were these.

Attached to the castle, but lying between it and the stepping-stones on the steep side of the hill, was an ancient enclosed orchard. It had doubtless been the original garden of the fortress, but the trees had gone back to their primitive "crabbiness" (as Hugh John put it), and in consequence the children were forbidden to eat any of the fruit—an order which might just as well not have been issued. But on a day it was reported to Janet Sheepshanks that Prissy and Hugh John were in the crab orchard. On tip-toe she stole down to catch them. She caught Hugh John. Prissy was up in one of the oldest and leafiest trees, and Hugh John, as in honour bound, persistently made signals in another direction to distract attention, as he was being hauled off to condign punishment.

He had an hour to wait in the study for his father, who was away at the county town. During this time Hugh John suffered strange qualms, not of apprehension, which presently issued in yet keener and more definitely located agony. At last Mr. Picton Smith entered.

"Well, sir, and what is this I hear?" he said severely, throwing down his riding-whip on the couch as if he meant to pick it up again soon.

Hugh John was silent. He saw that his father knew all there was to know about his evil doings from Janet Sheepshanks, and he was far too wise to plead guilty.

"Did I not tell you not to go to the orchard?"

Hugh John hung his head, and made a slight grimace at the pattern on the carpet, as a severer pang than any that had gone before assailed him.

"Now, look here, sir," said his father, shaking his finger at him in a solemnising manner, "If ever I catch you again in that orchard, I'll—I'll give you as sound a thrashing, sir, as ever you got in your life."

Hugh John rubbed his hand across his body just above the second lowest button of his jacket.

"Oh, father," he said plaintively, "I wish dreadfully that you had caught me before the last time I was in the orchard."

The treatment with pills and rhubarb which followed considerably retarded the operations of the army of Windy Standard. It was not the first time that the stomach of a commander-in-chief has had an appreciable effect on the conduct of a campaign.

CHAPTER XIII

THE ARMY OF WINDY STANDARD.

AT last, however, all was ready, in the historical phrase of Napoleon the Little, "to the last gaiter-button."

It was the intention of the Commander-in-Chief to attack the citadel of the enemy with banners flying, and after due notice. He had been practising for days upon his three-key bugle in order to give the call of Childe Roland. But Private Sammy Carter, who was always sticking his oar in, put him upon wiser lines, and (what is more) did it so quietly and suggestively that General Napoleon was soon convinced that Sammy's plan was his own, and on the second day boasted of its merits to its original begetter, who did not even smile. The like has happened in greater armies with generals as distinguished.

Sammy Carter advised that the assault should be delivered between eight and nine in the morning, for the very good reasons that at that hour both the butcher's apprentice, Tommy Pratt, and the slaughterman would be busy delivering the forenoon orders, while the butcher's son, Nipper Donnan, would be at school, and the Black Sheds consequently entirely deserted.

At first Hugh John rebelled, and asserted that this was not a sportsmanlike mode of proceeding, but Sammy Carter, who always knew more about everything than was good for anybody, overwhelmed his chief with examples of strategies and surprises from the military history of thirty centuries.

"Besides," said he, somewhat pertinently, "let's get Donald back first, and then we can be chivalrous all you want. Perhaps they are keeping him to fatten him up for the Odd Coons' Bank Holiday Feast."

This, as the wily Sammy knew, was calculated to stir up the wrath of his general more than anything else he could say. For at the annual Bean Feast of the Honourable Company of Odd Coons, a benefit secret society of convivial habits, a sheep was annually roasted whole. It said an ox on the programme, but the actual result, curiously enough, was mutton and not beef.

"We attack to-morrow at daybreak," said Field-Marshal Smith grandly, as soon as Sammy Carter had finished speaking.

This, however, had subsequently to be modified to nine o'clock, to suit the breakfast hour of the Carters. Moreover Saturday was substituted for Tuesday, both because Cissy and Sammy could most easily "shirk" their governess on that day, and because Mr. Picton Smith was known to be going up to London by the night train on Friday.

On such trivial circumstances do great events depend.

When the army was finally mustered for the assault, its armament was found to be somewhat varied, though generally efficient. But then even in larger armies the weapons of the different arms of the service are far from uniform. There are, for example, rifles and bayonets for the Line, lances for the Light Horse, carbines, sabres, and army biscuits, all deadly after their kind.

So it was in the campaigning outfit of the forces of Windy Standard. The historian can only hint at this equipment, so strange were the various kits. The Commander-in-Chief wished to insist on a red sash and a long cut-and-thrust sword, with (if possible) a kettle-drum. But this was found impracticable as a general order. For not only did the two divisional commanders decline to submit to the sash, but there were not enough kettle-drums intact to go more than half round.

So General Smith was the only soldier who carried a real sword. He had also a pistol, which, however, obstinately refused to go off, but formed a valuable weapon when held by the barrel. Cissy was furnished with a pike, constructed by Prince Michael's father, the dethroned monarch of O'Donowitch-dom, out of a leister or fish-spear—which, strangely enough, he had carried away with him from his palace at the time of his exile. This constituted a really formidable armament, being at least five feet long, and so sharp that if you ran very hard against a soft wooden door with it, it made a mark which you could see quite a yard off in a good light.

Prissy had a carpet-broom with a long handle, which at a distance looked like a gun, and as Prissy meant to do all her fighting at a distance this was quite sufficient. In addition she had three pieces of twine to tie up her dress, so that she would be ready to run away untrammelled by flapping skirts. Sir Toady Lion was equipped for war with a thimble, three sticky bull's-eyes, the haft of a knife (but no blade), a dog-whistle, and a go-cart with one shaft, all of which proved exceedingly useful.

The two Generals of Division were attired in neat stable clothes with buttoned leggings, and put their trust in a pair of "catties" (otherwise known as catapults), two stout shillelahs, the national batons of the exiled prince, manufactured by himself; and, most valuable of all, a set a-piece of horny knuckles, which they had kept in constant practice against each other all through the piping times of peace. Both Mike and Peter knowingly chewed straws in opposite corners of their mouths.

The forces on the other side were quite unknown, both as to number and quality. Hugh John maintained that there were at least twenty, and Toady Lion stoutly proclaimed that there were a million thousand, and that he had seen and counted them every one. But a stricter census, instituted upon evidence led by Private Sammy Carter, could not get beyond half-a-dozen. So that the disproportion was not so great as might have been supposed. Still the siege of the Sheds was felt to be of the nature of a forlorn hope.

It was arranged that all who distinguished themselves for deeds of valour were to receive the Victoria Cross, a decoration which had been cut by Hugh John out of the tops of ginger-beer bottles with a cold chisel. As soon, however, as Sir Toady Lion heard this, he sat down in the dust of the roadside, and simply refused to budge till his grievances were redressed.

"I wants Victowya Cyoss now!" he remarked, with his father's wrinkle of determination between the eyes showing very plain, as it always did when he wanted anything very much.

For when Toady Lion asked for a thing, like the person in the advertisement, he saw that he got it.

In vain it was pointed out to him that this ill-advised action constituted rank mutiny, and that he was liable to be arrested, tried by court-martial, and ignominiously shot. Toady Lion knew all about mutiny, and cared nothing about courts-martial. Besides, he had had some experience, and he knew the value of "making oneself a nuisance" in army matters.

Equally in vain was Sammy Carter's humorously false information that he had better run, for here was Janet coming up the road with an awful biggy stick.

"Don't care for Janet," reiterated Toady Lion. "I wants Victowya Cyoss—I wants it now!"

So there upon the roadside, at the very outset of the campaign, Sir Toady Lion was decorated with the much coveted "For Valour" cross.

And he would be a bold man who would say that he did not deserve it.

CHAPTER XIV

THE BATTLE OF THE BLACK SHEDS.

THIS much being settled, the army of Windy Standard advanced upon the enemy's entrenchments.

Prissy was the only soldier in the force with any religious convictions of a practical kind. On this occasion she actually wanted to send a mission to the foe with an offer of peace, on condition of their giving up Donald to his rightful owners. She instanced as an example of the kind of thing she meant, the verses about turning the other cheek. But General Napoleon had his answer ready.

"Well," he said, "that's all right. That's in the Bible, so I s'pose you have got to believe it. But I was looking at it last Sunday in sermon time, and it doesn't say what you are to do after you turn the other cheek. So yesterday I tried it on Tommy Pratt to see how it worked, and he hit me on the other cheek like winking, and made my eyes water. So then I took off my coat, and, Jove!— didn't I just give him Billy-O! Texts aren't so bad. They are mostly all right, if you only read on a bit!"

"But," said Prissy, "perhaps you forgot that a soft answer turneth away wrath?"

"Don't, nother," contradicted Sir Toady Lion, whose pronunciation of "wrath" and "horse" was identical, and who persistently misunderstood the Scriptural statement which Janet Sheepshanks had once made him learn without explanation. "Tried soft answer on big horse in the farm-yard, yesterday, and he didn't turn away a little bit, but comed right on, and tried to eat me all up!"

Toady Lion always had at least one word in italics in each sentence.

Prissy looked towards her ally and fellow-private for assistance.

"Love your——" suggested Sammy, giving her a new cue. Prissy thanked him with a look.

"Well," she said, "at least you won't deny that it says in the New Testament that you are to love your enemies!"

"I don't yike the New Test'ment," commented Toady Lion in his shrill high pipe, which cuts through all other conversation as easily as a sharp knife cleaves a bar of soap; "ain't never nobody killed dead in the New Test'ment!"

"Hush, Arthur George," said Prissy in a shocked voice, "you must not speak like that about the New Testament. It says 'Love your enemies!' 'Do good to them that hate you!' Now then!"

Hugh John turned away with a disgusted look on his face.

"Oh," he said, "of course, if you were to go on like that, there would never be any soldiers, nor bloody wars, nor nothing nice!"

Which of course would be absurd.

During this discussion the two Generals of Division had been wholly silent. To them the New Testament was considerably outside the sphere of practical politics. Peter Greg indeed had one which he had got from his mother on his birthday with his name on the first page; and Mike, who was of the contrary persuasion as to the advisability of circulating the Written Word in the vulgar tongue, could always provoke a fight by threatening to burn it, to which Peter Greg invariably replied by a hasty and ungenerous expression of hope as to the future welfare of the head of the Catholic religion.

But all this was purely academical discussion. Neither of them knew nor cared one jot about the matter. Prissy alone was genuinely distressed, and so affected was she that two big tears of woe trickled down her cheeks. These she wiped off with her pinafore, turning away her eyes so that Hugh John might not see them. There was, however, no great danger of this, for that warrior preoccupied himself with shouting "Right-left, Right-left," as if he were materially assisting the success of the expedition by doing so.

At the entrance to the pastures tenanted by butcher Donnan, the army divided into its two divisions under their several commanders. The Commander-in-Chief placed himself between the wings as a central division all by himself. It was Peter Greg who first reached the door, and with his stout cudgel knocked off the padlock. He had already entered in triumph, and was about to be followed by his soldiery, when a loud shout was heard from the edge of the park.

"Here they are—go at them! Give them fits, boys! We'll learn them to come sneaking into our field."

And over the stone dikes, from the direction of the town of Edam, came an overpowering force of the enemy led by Nipper Donnan. They seemed to arrive from all parts at once, and with sticks and stones they advanced upon the slender array of the forces of Windy Standard. Their rude language, their threatening gestures, and their loud shouts intimidated but did not daunt the assailants. Field-Marshal Napoleon Smith called on his men to do or die; and everyone resolved that that was just what they were there for—all except Prissy, who promptly pulled up her skirts and went down the meadow towards the stepping-stones like a jenny-spinner driven by the wind, and Sir Toady Lion, who, finding an opening in the hedge about his size in holes, crept quietly through and was immediately followed by Cæsar, the "potwalloping" Newfoundland pup.

The struggle which raged around those who remained staunch to the colours was grim and deadly. General-Field-Marshal Napoleon Smith threw himself into the thickest of the fray, and the cry, "A Smith for Merry England," alternated with the ringing "Scotland for ever!" which had so often carried terror into the hearts of the foe. Prince Michael O'Donowitch performed prodigies of valour, and personally "downed" three of the enemy with his national weapon. Peter Greg fought a pitched battle with Nipper Donnan, in which double-jointed words were as freely used as tightly clenched fists. Cissy Carter "progged" at least half-a-dozen of the enemy with her pike, before it was wrested from her by the united efforts of several town lads who were not going to stand being punched by a girl. Sammy Carter stood well out of the heady fray, and contented himself with stinging up the enemy with his vengeful catapult till they howled again.

"THE BATTLE OF THE BLACK SHEDS."

But the struggle of the many against the few, the strong against the weak, could only end in one way. In ten minutes the forces of law and disorder were scattered to the four quarters of heaven, and the standard that had streamed so rarely on the braes of Edam was in the hands of the exulting foe.

Prince Michael was wounded on the nose to the effusion of blood, General Peter Greg was a fugitive with a price on his head, and, most terrible of all—Field-Marshal Napoleon Smith was taken prisoner.

But Sir Toady Lion was neither among the slain, nor yet among the wounded or the captives. What then of Toady Lion?

CHAPTER XV

TOADY LION PLAYS A FIRST LONE HAND.

SIR Toady Lion had played a lone hand.

We left him sitting behind the hedge, secure as the gods above the turmoil of battle. But he could not be content to stay there. He thought of Richard Cœur-de-Lion, his great namesake and hero; and though he wanted to do nothing rash, he was resolved to justify the ginger-beer label Victoria Cross which he wore so proudly on his breast. So he waited till the forces of the town had swept those of Windy Standard from the field. He saw on the edge of the wood Hugh John, resisting manfully to the death, and striking out in all directions. But Toady Lion knew that he had no clear call to such very active exertions.

Cautiously he returned through his hole in the hedge, and crawling round the opposite side of the Black Sheds, he entered the door which Peter Greg had forced with his cudgel, before he had been interrupted by the arrival of the enemy. Toady Lion ran through a slippery byre in which calves had been standing, and came to an inner division with a low door and a causewayed floor like a pig-pen. He opened this gate by kicking up the hasp with the toe of his boot, and found himself at once in the inmost sanctuary.

And there, right before him, with a calf's halter of rope about his neck, all healthy and alive, was Donald, his own dear, black, pet lamb Donald, who gave a little bleat of pure delight upon seeing him, and pulled vigorously at the rope to get loose.

"Quiet now, Donald! Or they will come back. Stand still, 'oo horrid little beast 'oo, till I get the rope off!"

And so, easing the noose gradually, Toady Lion slipped it over Donald's head and he was free.

Then, very cautiously, his deliverer put his head round the door to see that the coast was clear. Not a soul was to be seen anywhere on the pastures; so Toady Lion slid out and made for the gap in the hedge, sure that Donald would follow him. Donald did follow, but, as luck would have it, no sooner was he through than Cæsar, who had been scraping for imaginary rabbits at the other side of the field, came barking and rushing about over the grass like a runaway traction engine.

Now Donald hated big dogs—they rugged and tugged his wool so; as soon therefore as he saw Cæsar he took down the lea towards the island as hard as he could go. He thundered across the wooden bridge, breaking through the fleeing forces of Windy Standard, which were scattered athwart the castle island. He sprinted over the short turf by the orchard, Cæsar lying off thirty yards on his flank. At the shallows by the stepping-stones Donald sheepfully took the water, and was not long in swimming to the other side, the Edam being hardly deep enough anywhere at this point to take him off his feet. In a minute more he was delightedly nuzzling his wet nose into the hand of Janet Sheepshanks, on the terrace of Windy Standard House.

"Wi beast, whaur hae ye come frae?—I declare I am that glad to see ye!"

But had she known the price which had been paid for Donald's liberty, her rejoicing would quickly have given place to sorrow. It was mid-afternoon on the day of battle and defeat when Toady Lion straggled home, so wet and dirty that he could only be slapped, bathed and sent to bed—which, in the absence of his father, was felt to be an utterly inadequate punishment.

Prissy had long ago fled home with a terrible tale of battle, murder, and sudden death. But she knew nothing of her brother Hugh John, though she had nerved herself to go back to the Black Sheds, suffering grinding agonies of fear and apprehension the while, as also of reproach for deserting him in his hour of need. Mike and Peter were quietly at work in the stable, in momentary dread of being called upon to give evidence.

The Carters, Sammy and Cissy, had run straight home, and were at that moment undoubtedly smelling of arnica and slimy with vaseline. But there was no trace of the Commander-in-Chief anywhere. General-Field-Marshal Napoleon Smith had vanished from the face of the earth.

"OH, THE BONNY LADDIE!"

Tea-time came and went. He had been known to be absent from tea. Supper-time arrived and overpassed, and then the whole house grew anxious. Ten o'clock came, and in the clear northern twilight all the household were scattered over the countryside seeking for him. Midnight, and no Hugh John! Where could he be? Drowned in the Edam Water—killed by a chance blow in the great battle—or simply hiding from fear of punishment and afraid to venture home? It must have been some stranger entirely unacquainted with General Napoleon Smith who advocated the last explanation. The inmates of Windy Standard cherished no such foolish hopes.

The sun rose soon after two on as glorious a summer morning as ever shone upon the hills of the Border. As his beams overshot Brown Gattonside to the east they fell on Janet Sheepshanks. Her decent white cap was green-moulded with the moss of the woods; the drip of waterside caves had grimed it, the cobwebs of murky outhouses festooned it. Her abundant grey hair hung down in untended witch locks. She had not shut an eye nor lain down all night.

Now she leaned her head on her hands and sobbed aloud.

"Oh, the bonny laddie! Whatever will I say to his faither when he comes hame? His auldest son and the aipple o' his e'e! My certie, if the ill-set loon were to come up the road the noo, I wad thresh the very skin aff his banes! To think that he should bide awa' like this. Oh, the dear, dear lamb that he is; and will thae auld e'en never mair rest on his bonnie face? Cauld, cauld noo it looks up frae the bottom o' some pool in the Edam Water!"

And Janet Sheepshanks, like one of the mothers in Ramah, lifted up her voice and wept with the weeping which will not be comforted; for oft-times bairns' play brings that which is not bairns' play to those who love them.

CHAPTER XVI

THE SMOUTCHY BOYS.

GENERAL Napoleon Smith had been taken captive by the Comanche Cowboys. Now it is fair to say in this place that they also had their side of the question. Their fathers were, in their own opinion, striving for the ancient rights of the town against an interloping Smith. Why should not they against the son of that Smith and his allies? The denunciations of the Edam Town Council were only transformed into the blows which rained down so freely upon Hugh John's bare and curly head, as he stood at bay that Saturday morning in the corner of the dike.

"Surrender!" cried Nipper Donnan, whose father had moved that the town of Edam take the case up to the House of Lords.

"'A Smith dies but does not surrender'!" replied the son of the man who had declared his intention of fighting the matter out though it took his last copper.

In the calm atmosphere of the law-courts this was very well, and the combatants stood about an equal chance; but not so when translated into terms to suit the Black Sheds of Edam and the links of the castle island.

So the many-headed swarmed over the wall from behind; they struck down the last brave defender of privilege, and Hugh John Picton Smith was borne away to captivity.

Now there are many tongues and many peoples on the face of the earth, and doubtless the one Lord made them all. But there is one variety which appears among all nations, and commentators disagree as to what particular Power is responsible for his creation. He is the Smoutchy Boy.

This universal product of the race is indeed the chief evidence that we are lineally connected with the brutes that perish; for there is no doubt that the Smoutchy Boy is a brute among brutes. He is at once cruel and cowardly, boastful and shy, ready to strike a weaker, and equally ready to cry out when a stronger strikes him. He is not peculiar to any one class of society. He frequents the best public-schools, and is responsible for the under-current of cruelty which ever and anon rises to the surface there and supplies a month's free copy to enterprising journals in want of a sensation for the dull season. He makes some regiments of the service a terror. He understands all about "hazing" in the navy. Happily, however, among such large collections of human beings there is generally some clear-eyed, upstanding, able-bodied, long-armed Other Product who, by way of counterpoise, has been specially created to be the defender of the oppressed, and the scourge of the Smoutchy Boy.

I have seen one such scatter a dozen Smoutchies, who were employed after their kind in stoning to death a nestful of fluffy, gaping, yellow-billed young blackbirds. I have heard the sound of his fists striking most compactly and satisfactorily against Smoutchy flesh. Also I know the jar with which a foot stops suddenly in mid-air, as the Scourge pursues and kicks the fleeing Smoutchy—kicks him "for keeps" too.

Yet for all this Smoutchy Boy is a man and a brother. His smoutchiness generally passes off with the callowness of hobble-de-hoyhood. The condition is indeed rather one for the doctor than for the Police Court. It is pathological rather than criminal; for when the Smoutchy is thrown for some time into the society of men of the world—drilled for instance in barrack yards, licked and clouted into shape by the regiment or the ship's crew, he sheds his smoutchiness from him like a garment. It is on record that Smoutchies ere now have led forlorn hopes, pierced Africa to its centre, navigated strange seas, and trodden trackless Polar snows. The worst Smoutchy of my time, the bully who, till the biceps and tendo Achilles muscles hardened to their office, made life at a certain school a terror and an agony, afterwards sprang from a steamer in order to save the life of a man who had fallen overboard in a high-running sea.

"THE HEAD SMOUTCHY."

But of all Smoutchies the worst variety is that reared in the vicinity of the small manufacturing town. He thrives on wages too early and too easily earned. Foul language, a tobacco pipe with the bowl turned down, and the rotten fagends of Association football, are the signs by which you may know him. In such a society there is always one Smoutchy who sets the fashion, and a crowd who imitate.

In Edam the head Smoutchy of the time was Nipper Donnan. He was the son of a fighting butcher, who in his day, and before marrying the widow of the deceased publican of the "Black Bull," had been a yet more riotous drover, and had almost met the running expenses of the Sheriff Court by his promptly paid fines.

The only things Nipper Donnan feared were the small, round, deep-set eyes of his father. The police were a sport to him. The well-brought-up children of the Grammar School trembled at his name. The rough lads at work in the mills on the Edam Water almost worshipped him; for it was known that his father gave him lessons in pugilism. He sported a meerschaum pipe; a spotted handkerchief was always knotted knowingly round his throat, and a white bull-dog, with red sidelong eyes and lips drawn up at the corners, followed close at his heel.

Great in Edam and on all the banks of the Edam Water was Nipper Donnan, the King of the Smoutchies.

And it was into his hard, rough, unclean hands that our brave General Napoleon had fallen. Now Nipper had been reared in special hatred of the Smiths of Windy Standard. Mr. Picton Smith it was who, long ago at Edam Fair, as a young man, had interfered with Drover Donnan, when he was just settling to "polish off" a soft, good-natured shepherd of the hills, whom he had failed to cheat out of the price of his "blackfaces." Mr. Picton Smith it was who on the same occasion had sentenced the riotous drover to "thirty days without the option of a fine." He it was in times more recent who had been the means of getting the Black Bull shut up, upon the oft-repeated complaint of the Chief Constable.

And so all this heritage of hatred was now to be worked off on the son of the gentleman by the son of the bully. Of course it might just as well have been the other way about, for there is no absolute heredity in Smoutchydom. The butcher might easily have been the gentleman, and the landlord's son the Smoutchy bully; only to Hugh John's cost, on this occasion it happened to be the other way about.

The lads who followed Nipper Donnan were mostly humble admirers—some more cruel, some less, but sworn Smoutchies to a man, and all afraid to interfere with the fierce pleasures of their chief. Indeed, so absolute was Captain Nipper Donnan, that there never was a time when some of his band did not bear the marks of his attentions.

CHAPTER XVII

BEFORE THE INQUISITION.

WITH this excursion into the natural history of the Smoutchy Boy, which perhaps ought to have come somewhat earlier in the history, we continue the tale of the adventures of General Napoleon Smith.

Beaten down by numbers, the hero lay on the ground at the corner of the butcher's parks. Nipper Donnan stood over him and held him down with his foot. They were just the right ages for bully and bullied. Hugh John Smith was twelve, slim, and straight as an arrow; Nipper Donnan sixteen, short, hard, and thick set, with large solid hands and prominent knuckles.

"Got you at last, young prig! Now I'll do you to rights!" remarked Nipper, genially kicking Hugh John in the ribs with his hobnailed boots.

Hugh John said not a word, for he had fought till there was no more breath left in him anywhere.

"Sulky, hey?" said Nipper, with another kick in a more tender spot. Hugh John winced. "Ah, lads, I thought that would wake the young swell up. Oh, our father is the owner of this property, is he? So nice! He owns the town, does he? Nasty pauper he is! Too poor to keep a proper carriage, but thinks us all dirt under his feet. Yaw, yaw, we aw-w so fine, we aw-w, we a-aw!"

And Nipper Donnan imitated, amid the mean obsequious laughter of his fighting tail, the erect carriage of his father's enemy, Mr. Picton Smith, as he was accustomed to stride somewhat haughtily down the High Street of Edam.

Then he came back and kicked Hugh John again.

"You wouldn't dare to do this if my father were here!" said General Napoleon, now sitting up on his elbow.

"Your father, I'll show you!" shouted furiously Nipper the Tyrant. "Who asked you to come here anyway to meddle with us? Who invited you into our parks? What business have you in our castle? Fetch him along, boys; we'll show him something that neither he nor his father know anything about. They and the likes of them used to shut up people in the castle dungeons, so they say. We are just the boys to give 'em a taste of what it is like theirselves."

"Hooray," shouted the Smoutchy fighting tail; "fetch him along, lads!"

So with no gentle hands Hugh John was seized and hurried away. He was touched up with ironbound clogs in the rear, his arms were pinched underneath where the skin is tender, as well as nearly dragged from their sockets. A useless red cravat was thrust into his mouth by way of a gag—useless, for the prisoner would sooner have died than have uttered one solitary cry.

And all the time Hugh John was saying over and over to himself the confession of his faith:

"I'm glad I didn't tell—I'm glad I wasn't 'dasht-mean.' I'm a soldier. The Scots Greys saluted me; and these fellows shan't make me cry."

And they didn't. For the spirit of many generations of stalwart Smiths and fighting Pictons was in him, and perhaps also a spark from the ancestral anvil of the first Smith had put iron into his boyish blood. So all through the scene which followed—the slow mock trial, the small ingenious tortures, pulling back middle fingers, hanging up by thumbs to a beam with his toes just touching the ground, tying a string about his head and tightening it with a twisted stick—Hugh John never cried a tear, which was the bitterest drop in the cup of Nipper Donnan.

They removed the gag in order that they might question him.

"Say this is not your father's castle, and we'll let you down!" cried Nipper.

"It is my father's and nobody else's! And when it is mine, I shan't let one of you beasts come near it."

The Smoutchies tried another tack.

"Promise you won't tell on us if we let you go!"

"I shan't promise; I will tell every one of your names to the policeman, and get you put in jail—so there! My father has gone to London to see the Queen, and have you all put into prison—yes, and whipped with a cat-o'-nine-tails as soon as ever he comes back!" answered Hugh John, shamelessly belying both his father and his own intentions.

But he comforted himself and excused the lie, by saying to himself, "It is none of their business whether I tell on them or not. They shan't think that I don't tell because I am afraid of them!"

And the great heart of the hero (aged twelve) stood high and unshaken.

At last even Nipper Donnan tired of the cruel sport. It was no great fun when the victim could not be made to cry or appeal for mercy. And even the fighting tail grew vaguely restive, perhaps becoming indistinctly conscious, in spite of their blind admiration for their chief, that by comparison with the steadfast defiance and upright mien of their solitary victim, the slouching, black-pipe-smoking smoutchiness of Nipper Donnan did not appear the truly heroic figure.

"Let's put him in the dungeon, and leave him there! I can come and let him out after, and then kick the beggar home the way he came! That will learn him to let us alone for ever and ever!"

The fighting tail shouted agreement, and Hugh John was promptly haled to the mouth of the prison-house; a rope was rove about his waist, his hands were tied behind his back, and he was lowered down into the ancient dungeon of the Castle of Windy Standard. This place of confinement had last been used a hundred and fifty years ago for the stragglers of the Bonny Prince's army after the retreat northward. The dungeon was bottle-necked above, and spread out beneath into a circular vault of thirty or forty feet in diameter. Its depth was about twelve feet; and as the boys had not rope enough to lower their prisoner all the way, they had perforce to let Hugh John drop, and he lighted on his feet, taking of course the rope with him.

"Come on, lads," cried Nipper Donnan, "let's go and have a smoke at the Black Sheds, and then go up to the Market Hill to see the shows. The proud swine will do well enough down there till his father comes back from London with the cat-o'-nine-tails!"

He looked over the edge and spat into the dungeon.

"That for you!" he cried. "Will ye say now that the castle is your father's, and that we have no right here!"

Hugh John tried to give the required information as to ownership, but it was choked in the folds of the red cravat. Nipper went on tauntingly, all unchallenged.

"'WILL YE SAY NOW THAT THE CASTLE IS YOUR FATHER'S, AND THAT WE HAVE

NO RIGHT HERE!' SAID NIPPER DONNAN."

"There's ethers (adders) down there—and weasels and whopper rats that eat off your fingers and toes. Yes, and my father saw a black beast like an otter, but as big as a calf, run in there out of the Edam Water; and they'll bite ye and stang ye and suck your blood! And we are never coming back no more, so ye'll die of starvation besides."

With this pleasing speech by way of farewell and benediction, Nipper Donnan drew off his forces, and Hugh John was left alone.

CHAPTER XVIII

THE CASTLE DUNGEON.

FOR some time after Hugh John was thus imprisoned, he stood looking up with a face of set defiance through the narrow aperture above, where he had last seen the triumphant countenances of his foes.

"Who's afraid? They shan't say Hugh John Picton Smith is afraid!" were the words in his proud and angry heart, which kept him from feeling insult and pain, kicks and buffetings. Gradually, however, as the sound of retreating footsteps died away, the rigid attitude of the hero relaxed. He began to be conscious that he was all one great ache, that the ropes were drawn exceedingly tight about his wrists, that the gag in his mouth hurt his cheeks, that he was very tired—and, oh! shame for a hero of battles and martyr in secret torture-chambers, that he wanted badly to sit down and cry.

"But I won't cry—even to myself!" said Hugh John. Yet all the same he sat mournfully down to consider his position. He did not doubt that he had been left there for altogether, and he began at once (perhaps to keep himself from crying) to argue out the chances.

"First," he said, "I must wriggle my hands loose, then I can get the gag out of my mouth easy enough. After that I've got to count my stores, and see if I can find a rusty nail to write my name on the wall and the date of my captivity."

(Hugh John wanted to do everything decently and in order.)

"Then I must find a pin or a needle (a needle if possible—a pin is poisonous, and besides it is so much more easy to prick blood from your thumb with a needle), and then I have got to write an account of my sufferings on linen like the abbé, or on tablets of bread like Latude. As I have no bread, except the lump that was left over at breakfast, I suppose it will need to be written on linen; but bread tablets are much the more interesting. Of course I could make one or two tablets, write secret messages on them, and eat them after."

General Smith would have gone on to make still further arrangements for the future, but the present pain of the blood in his hands and the tightness of the rope at his wrists warned him that he had better begin the practical work of effecting his release.

Now General Smith was not one of that somewhat numerous class of persons who take all day to do nothing, and as soon as he was convinced by indisputable logic of the wisdom of any course, he threw himself heart and soul into the accomplishment of it. On his hands and knees he went half round the circuit of the wall of his prison, but encountered nothing save the bare clammy stones—with the mortar loose and crumbly in the joints, and the moist exudations of the lime congealed into little stony blobs upon the surface which tasted brackish when he put his lips to them.

So Hugh John stood up and began a new search on another level. This time he did find something to the purpose.

About three feet from the ground was a strong nail driven firmly into a joint of the masonry. Probably it owed its position to one of the Highland prisoners of the Forty-five, who had used it to hang his spare clothes on, or for some other purpose. But in his heart Hugh John dated it from the days of the Black Douglas at least.

Either way it proved most useful.

Standing with his back to the wall, the boy could just reach it with his wrists. He had long thin hands with bones which, when squeezed, seemed to have a capacity for fitting still more closely into one another. So it was not difficult for him to open the palms sufficiently to let the head of the nail in. Then biting his teeth upon his lip to keep the pain at a bearable point, he bent the weight of his body this way and that upon the iron pin, so that in five or six minutes he had worked Nipper Donnan's inartistic knots sufficiently loose to slip over his wrists. His hands were free.

"HE BENT THE WEIGHT OF HIS BODY THIS WAY AND THAT."

His first act was to take the red cravat out of his mouth, and the next after that to lie down with all his weight upon his hands, holding them between the floor of the dungeon and his breast, for the tingling pain of the blood returning into the fingers came nearer to making the hero cry than all that had happened that day. But he still refrained.

"No, I won't, I am a Napoleon—Smith!" he added as an afterthought, as if in loyalty to the father, whose legal and territorial claims he had that day so manfully upheld.

But suddenly what was due to his dignified position as a state prisoner occurred to him. Casanova had struck at the wall till his fingers bled. Latude had gnashed his teeth, howled with anguish, and gnawed the earth.

"I have not done any of these things," said Hugh John; "I don't like it. But I suppose I've got to try!"

However, one solid rap of his knuckles upon the hard limestone of the dungeon wall persuaded him that there were things more amusing in the world than to imitate Casanova in that. And as at the first gnaw his mouth encountered a tiny nettle, he leaped to his feet and declared at the pitch of his voice that both Latude and Casanova were certainly "dasht fools!"

The sound of his own words reminded him that after all he was within a mile of home. He wondered what time it might be. He began to feel hungry, and the cubic capacity of his internal emptiness persuaded him that it must be at least quite his usual dinner-time.

So Hugh John decided that, all things being considered, it would be nothing against his manhood if he called for help, and took his chance of any coming. But he remembered that the mouth of the dungeon was in a very retired part of the castle, in the wing nearest to the river, and shut off from the road across the island by a flanking tower and a thirteen-foot wall. So he was not very sanguine of success. Still he felt that in his perilous position he could not afford to neglect any chance, however slight.

So he shouted manfully, "Help! Help! Murder! Police! Fire!" as loud as he could bawl.

Then he tried the "Coo-ee" which Sergeant Steel had taught him, under the impression that it would carry farther. But the keep of a fourteenth century castle and thirteen feet of shell lime and rubble masonry are proof against the most willing boyish voice in the world. So General Napoleon made no more impression upon his friends than his great original would have done had he summoned the Old Guard from the cliffs of St. Helena.

But the younger warrior was not discouraged. He had tried one plan and it had failed. He sat down again to think what was the next thing to be done.

He remembered the thick "hunk" of bread he had put in the pocket of his jacket in the morning. He could not eat it at breakfast, so greatly had he been excited by the impending conflict; so, to prevent waste, and to make all safe, he had put it in his pocket. Besides, in the absence of his father, it was not always possible to be in for meals. And—well, one never knew what might happen. It was best to be prepared for all emergencies.

With trembling hand he felt for the "hunk." Alas! the jacket pocket was empty, and hung flat and limp against his side. The staff of life must have fallen out in the progress of the fray, or else one of the enemy had despoiled him of his treasure.

A quick thought struck his military mind, accustomed before all else to deal with questions of commissariat. It was just possible that the bread might have fallen out of his pocket when the Smoutchies were letting him down so roughly into the dungeon of the castle.

He went directly underneath the aperture, from which a faint light was distributed over the uneven floor of hard trampled earth whereon a century's dry dust lay ankle deep.

There—there, almost under his feet, was his piece of bread!

Hugh John picked it up, blew the dust carefully off, and wiped the surface with his handkerchief. It was a good solid piece of bread, and would have served Cæsar the Potwalloper for at least two mouthfuls. With care it might sustain life for an indefinite period—perhaps as much as twenty-four hours.

So, in accordance with the best traditions, the prisoner divided his provision with his pocketknife, as accurately as possible under the circumstances. He cut it into cubes of about an inch square, exactly as if he had been going to lay down rat poison.

Napoleon Smith was decidedly beginning to recover his spirits. For one thing, he thought how very few boys had ever had his chances. A Latude of twelve was somewhat unusual in the United Kingdom of Great Britain and Ireland, and even in the adjacent islands. He began at once to write his memoirs in his head, but found that he could not get on very well, because he could not remember which one of his various great-grandmothers had danced with Bonny Prince Charlie at Edinburgh. This for a loyal prisoner was insuperable, so he gave the memoirs up.

CHAPTER XIX

THE DROP OF WATER.

FROM fruitless genealogy he turned to the further consideration of his supplies. He wanted water, and in a dungeon surrounded by lime-stone walls and founded upon a rock, it seemed likely he would continue to want it. But at the farthest corner, just where the roof approached most closely to the floor, Hugh John could hear a pat, pat at regularly recurring intervals. He put his hand forward into the darkness, and immediately a large drop of water fell on the back of it. He set his tongue to it, and it tasted cool and good after the fustiness of the woollen gag.

Hugh John thrust forward his hand again, palm upwards this time, and was rewarded by finding that every time he counted ten slowly a large drop, like those in the van of a thunder storm, splashed into the hollow. It was tedious work, but then a dungeon is a slow place, and he had plenty of time. He crawled forward to be nearer to the source of supplies, and while trying to insinuate his head sideways underneath like a dog at a spout, to catch the drop in his mouth without the intervention of a warm hand, he felt that his knee was wet. He had inadvertently placed it in a small natural basin into which the drop had been falling for ages. Hugh John set his lips to it, and never did even soda-water-and-milk, that nectar of the meagre and uncritical gods of boyhood, taste sweeter or more refreshing. After he had taken a good solid drink he cleaned the sand from the bottom carefully, and there, ready to his hand, was a stone cup hollowed out of a projecting piece of the rock on which the castle was built. This well-anchored drinking-cup was shaped like the pecten-shell of pilgrimage, and set with the broad fluted end towards him.

Thus fortified with meat and drink, for he had devoured the first of his rat-poison squares, or rather bolted it like a pill, General Napoleon sat down to reckon up his resources. He found himself in possession of some ten feet of fairly good cord, which had evidently been used for bringing cattle to the fatal Black Sheds of butcher Donnan. The prisoner carefully worked out all the knots, in order to get as much length as possible. He did not, indeed, see how such a thing could help him to escape, but that was not his business, for in the authorities a rope was always conveyed into the cell of the pining captive, generally in an enormous pie.

Hugh John felt that he was indeed a pining captive, but it was the pie and not the rope he pined for. His dungeon was downstairs, and he did not see how a rope could possibly help him to get out, unless there was somebody at the top of the bottle ready to haul him up.

He tried his voice again, and made the castle ring in vain. Alas! only the echoes came back, the pert jackdaws cried out insolently far above him and mocked him in a clamorous crowd from the ruined gables.

Then his mind went off all of itself to the pleasant dining-room of the house of Windy Standard, where Prissy and Sir Toady Lion would even now be sitting down to tea. He could smell the nice refreshing bouquet of the hot china pot as Janet Sheepshanks poured the tea into the cups in a golden brown jet, and then "doused" in the cream with a liberal hand.

"I declare I could drink up the whole tea-pot full without ever stopping," said Hugh John aloud, and then started at the sound of his own voice.

He waited as long as possible, and then ate the second of his squares of bread. Then he drank the mouthful of water which had gathered in the stone shell. While he was in there underneath the dungeon eaves, he put out his hand to feel how far off the wall was. He expected easily to reach it, but in this he failed entirely. His hand was merely stretched out into space, while the drop fell upon his head, and then upon his neck, as he leaned farther and farther over in his efforts to find a boundary wall.

He had noticed from the first that the floor immediately beneath the cup was quite dry all round, but it had not occurred to him before that if the drop fell constantly and regularly the basin must overflow in some direction. Hugh John was not logical. It is true that he liked finding out things by his five senses, but then that is a very different affair. Sammy Carter tried to argue with him sometimes, and make matters clear to him by pure reason. The first time Hugh John usually told him to "shut it." The second he simply hammered the logician.

Finally, to solve the mystery, Hugh John crawled completely over his drinking fountain and kneeled in the damp sand at the back of the basin. Still he could discover no wall. Next, he put his hand forward as far as it would reach out, and—he could feel no floor.

Very gingerly he put his foot over the edge, and at once found himself on the top step of a steep, narrow, and exceedingly uneven stair. The explorer's heart beat fast within him. He knew what it was now that he had found—a secret passage, perhaps ending in an enchanted cave; perhaps (who knew) in a pirate's den. He thought of Nipper Donnan's last words about the beast as big as a calf which his father had seen going down into the dungeon. It was a lie, of course; it must be, because Nipper Donnan said it; but still it was certainly very dark and dismal down there.

Hugh John listened with his ear pointed down the stair, and his mouth open. He certainly did hear a low, rushing, hissing sound, which might be the Edam water surrounding the old tower, or—the breathing of the Black Beast.

If Hugh John had had even Toady Lion with him, he would have felt no fears; but to be alone in silence and darkness is fitted to shake stronger nerves than those of a twelve-year-old boy. It was getting late, as he knew by the craving ache in his stomach, and also by the gradual dusking of the hole twelve feet above his head, through whose narrow throat he had been let down in the forenoon.

Now at first the Smoutchy boys had not meant to leave Hugh John in the dungeon all night, but only to give him a thorough fright for his hardihood in daring to attack their citadel. But Nipper Donnan's natural resolution was ever towards cruelty of all sorts, and it was turned to adamant upon discovering that Donald, the captured hostage and original cause of conflict, had in some mysterious way escaped.

This unexpected success of the attacking party he attributed, of course, to Hugh John, whom, in spite of his youth, he well knew to be the leading spirit. Sir Toady Lion was never so much as suspected—a fact which would have pleased that doughty warrior but little had he known it.

In the afternoon Nipper had gone to Halkirk Tryst to bring home two bullocks, which Butcher Donnan had bought there the day before; but his father becoming involved in some critical cattle-dealing transaction, for which he was unable to obtain satisfaction in cash, resolved that Nipper should wait till the next day, when he hoped to be able to accompany him home in person. So engrossed was Nipper with the freaks of the fair, the Aunt-Sallies, the shooting-galleries, and miscellaneous side-shows and ghost illusions, that he quite forgot all about our hero immured in the dungeon of the Castle of Windy Standard. Even had he remembered, he would certainly have said to himself that some of the other boys would be sure to go and let him out (for which interference with his privileges he would assuredly punch their heads to-morrow!)—and that in any case it served the beggar right.

Probably, however, his father (had Nipper thought fit to mention the matter to him), would have taken quite a different view of the situation; for the butcher, with all his detestation of the owner of the Windy Standard estate, held Mr. Picton Smith in a wholesome awe which almost amounted to reverence.

So it came about that none approached the castle all that afternoon; for the boys of Nipper's band were afraid to venture upon the castle island in the absence of their redoubtable chief, while the servants of Windy Standard House sought for the vanished in quite other directions, being led astray by the innocent assertions of Toady Lion, who had last seen Hugh John defending himself gallantly against overwhelming numbers in the corner of the field nearest to the town, and at least half a mile as the crow flies from the castle on the island.

CHAPTER XX

THE SECRET PASSAGE.

FOR a full hour Hugh John sat on the top step of the stairs, or went back and forward between these and the narrow circular opening so high above his head, which was now filled with a sort of ruddy haze, the sign that the sun was setting comfortably and sedately outside, behind the smooth green hills in which the Cheviots broke down into the Solway Marshes. It was not so much that the boy dared not descend into the secret passage. Rather he did not wish to confront the blankness of disappointment. The steps might lead nowhere at all. They might drop off suddenly into the depths of a well.

To prove to himself that he was quite calm, and also that he was in no hurry, Hugh John ate the third of his bread-squares and drank the water which had meantime collected in the stone shell. Heroes always refreshed themselves thus before an adventure.

"'None knoweth when our lips shall touch the blessed bread again!' This prog's too hanged dry for anything!"—that was what Hugh John said, quoting (partly) from the "Life and Death of Arthur the King."

Then feeling that mere poetry was off and that the time for action had definitely come, he tied to his rope a large fallen stone which lay in a corner, and crawling over the shell to the head of the steps, he threw it down. It did not go far, appearing to catch in some projection. He tried again with a like result. He pulled it up. The stone was dry. The opening was not, then, a well with water at the bottom.

So Hugh John cautiously put his foot upon the threshold of the secret passage, and commenced the perilous descent. He clutched the edge of the top step as he let himself down. It was cold, wet, and clammy, but the stones beneath seemed secure enough. So he continued to descend till he found himself in a narrow staircase which went down and down, gradually twisting to the left away from the light. His heart beat fast, and there was a curious heavy feeling about his nostrils, which doubtless came from the damp mists of a confined place so close to the river.

The adventurous General had descended quite a long way when he came to a level stone-flagged passage. He advanced twenty yards along it, and then put out his hands. He found himself in a narrow cell, dripping with wet and ankle deep in mud. The cell was so small, that by making a couple of steps Hugh John could feel it from side to side. At the farther end of it there was evidently a door or passage of some sort, but it was blocked up with fallen stones and rubbish; yet through it came the strangest muffled noises. Something coughed like a man in pain. There was also a noise as of the feet of animals moving about stealthily and restlessly, and he seemed even to hear voices speaking.

A wild unreasoning fear suddenly filled the boy's heart. He turned and fled, stumbling hastily up the stairs by which he had so cautiously descended. The thought of the black beast, great as a calf, of which Nipper Donnan had spoken, came upon him and almost mastered him. Yet all the time he knew that Nipper had only said it to frighten him. But it was now dark night, even in the upper dungeon. He was alone in a haunted castle, and, as the gloaming settled down, Hugh John cordially agreed with Sir David Brewster, who is reputed to have said, "I do not believe in ghosts, but I am afraid of them."

In spite of all his gallantry of the day, and the resolutions he had made that his prison record should be strictly according to rule, Hugh John's sudden panic took complete hold of him. He sat down under the opening of the dungeon, and for the first time cried bitter tears, excusing himself on the ground that there was no one there to see him, and anyway he could easily leave that part out when he came to write his journal. About this time he also slipped in a surreptitious prayer. He thought that at least it could do no harm. Prissy had induced him to try this method sometimes, but mostly he was afraid to let her know about it afterwards, because it made Prissy so unbearably conceited. But after all this was in a dungeon, and many very respectable prisoners quite regularly said their prayers, as any one may see for themselves in the books.

"You see," said Hugh John, explanatorily afterwards, "it's very easy for them. They have nothing else to do. They haven't to wash, and take baths, and comb their hair, and be ordered about! It's easy to be good when you're leading a natural life."

This was Hugh John's prayer, and a model for any soldier's pocket-book.

"Our Father Witch-Charta-Nevin" (this he considered a Christian name and surname, curious but quite authoritative), "help me to get out of this beastly hole. Help me to lick Nipper Donnan till he can't stand, and bust Sammy Carter for running away. For we are all miserable sinners. God bless father and Prissy, Arthur George (I wonder where the little beast went to—guess he sneaked—just wait!), Janet Sheepshanks, Mary Jane Housemaid, and everybody about the house and down at the stables, except Bella Murdoch, that is a clash-bag and a tell-tale-tit. And make me a good boy. For Jesus' sake. Aymen."

That the last petition was by no means a superfluous one every reader of this history will agree. Hugh John very carefully said "Ay-men" now, because he had said "A-men" in the morning. He noticed that his father always said "Ay-men" very solemnly at the end of a prayer, while Prissy, who liked going to church even on week days (a low dodge!), insisted upon "A-men." So Hugh John used "Ay-men" and "A-men" time about, just to show that there was no ill-feeling. Thus early in life does the leaven of Gallio (who "cared for none of these things") begin to show itself. Hugh John was obviously going to be a very pronounced Broad Churchman.

The prayer did the captive General much good. He was not now nearly so much afraid of the beasts. The hole did not seem to yawn so black beneath him; and though he kept his ear on the cock for anything that might come at him up the stairs, he could with some tolerable composure sit still and wait for the morning. He decided that so soon as it was even a little light, he would try again and find out if he could not remove the rubbish from the further door.

The midsummer morn was not long in coming—shorter far indeed to Hugh John than to the anxious hearts that were scattered broadcast over the face of the country seeking for him. Scarcely had the boy sat down to wait for the daylight when his head sank on his breast. Presently he swayed gently to the side, and turning over with a contented little murmur, he curled himself up like a tired puppy and went fast asleep. When he awoke, a fresher pink radiance than that of eventide filled the aperture above his head—the glow of the wide, sweet, blushful dawn which flooded all the eastern sky outside the tall grey walls of the Castle of Windy Standard.

Hugh John rose, stretched himself, yawned, and looked about him in surprise. There was no Toady Lion in a little white ship on four iron legs, moored safe alongside him; no open door through into Prissy's room; no birch-tree outside the window, glimmering purest white and delicatest pink in the morning light—nothing, in short, that had greeted his waking eyes every morning of his life hitherto.

But there were compensations. He was a prisoner. He had endured a night in a dungeon. His hair would almost certainly have turned pure white, or at least streaky. What boy of his age had ever done these things since the little Dauphin, about whom he was so sorry, and over whose fate he had shed such bitter tears? Had Sammy Carter? Hugh John smiled a sarcastic and derisive smile. Sammy Carter indeed! He would just like to see Sammy Carter try it once! He would have been dead by this time, if he had had to go through the tenth of what he (Hugh John) had undergone. Had Mike or Peter? They were big and strong. They smoked pipes. But they had never been tortured, never shut up in a dungeon with wild beasts in the next compartment, and no hasp on the door.

The staircase—the secret passage! Hugh John's heart fluttered wildly. He might even yet get back in time for breakfast. There would be porridge—and egg-and-bacon—oh! crikey, yes, and it was kidney morning. Hugh John's mouth watered. There was no need of the cool fluid in the shell of limestone now! Could there indeed be such dainties in the world? It did not seem possible. And yet that very morning—he meant the morning before—no, surely it must have been in some other life infinitely remote, he had grumbled because he had not had cream instead of milk to his porridge, and because the bacon was not previously crisp enough. He felt that if ever he were privileged to taste as good bacon again, he would become religious like Prissy—or take some such extreme measure as that.

"OVER THE CLOSELY PACKED WOOLLY BACKS HE SAW A STRETCH OF RIPPLED RIVER."

Hugh John had no appetite for the "poison squares" now. He tried one, and it seemed to be composed in equal parts of sawdust and the medicament called "Rough-on-rats!" He tried the water in the shell, and that was somewhat better; but just to think of tea from the urn—soft ivory cream floating on the top, curded a little but light as blown sea-foam! Ah, he could wait no longer. The life of a prisoner was all very well, but he could not even get materials with which to write up his diary till he got home. For this purpose it was necessary that he should immediately make his escape. Also it was kidney morning, and if he did not hurry that little wretch Toady Lion would have eaten up every snatch. He resolved to lose no time.

So with eager steps he descended the steep wet stairs into the little stone chamber, which smelt fearfully damp and clammy, just as if all the snails in the world had been crawling there.

"I bet the poor chap down here had toothache," said Hugh John, shivering as he went forward to attack the pile of fallen stones in front of the arched doorway. For an hour he worked most manfully, pulling out such as he could manage to loosen, and tossing others aside. Thus he gradually undercut the mass which blocked up the door, till, with a warning creak or two the whole pitched forward and inward, giving the daring pioneer just time to leap aside before it came toppling into the narrow cell, which it more than half filled. As soon as the avalanche had settled, Hugh John staggered over the top of the fallen stones and broken débris to the small door. As his head came on a level with the opening he saw a strange sight. He looked into a little ruined turret, the floor of which was of smoothest green sward—or, rather, which would have been of green sward had it not been thickly covered with sheep, all lying placidly shoulder to shoulder, and composedly drawing in the morning air through their nostrils as if no such word as "mutton" existed in the vocabularies of any language.

Beyond and over the closely packed woolly backs he saw a stretch of rippled river, faceted with diamond and ruby points, where the rising sun just touched the tips of the little chill wavelets which were fretted by the wind of morning, that gust of cooler air which the dawn pushes before it round the world. Hugh John was free!

CHAPTER XXI

THE RETURN FROM THE BASTILE.

HE stepped down easily and lightly among the sheep. They rose without surprise or disorder, still with strict attention to business continuing to munch at the grass they had plucked as they lay, for all the world as if a famous adventure-seeking general had been only the harmless but boresome shepherd who came to drive them out to pastures new. For all the surprise they showed they might have been accustomed from their fleeciest infancy to small, dirty, scratched, bruised, infinitely tattered imps of imperial descent arriving suddenly out of unexplored secret passages in ancient fortresses.

The great commander's first instinct was to rush for home and so make sure that Cook Mary the Second had done enough kidneys for breakfast. His second idea, and one more worthy of his military reputation, was carefully to conceal the entrance to the doorway, by which he had emerged from the passage he had so wonderfully discovered. No one knew how soon the knowledge might prove useful to him. As a matter of attack and defence the underground passage was certainly not to be neglected.

Then Hugh John drove the sheep before him out of the fallen tower. As he did so one of them coughed, stretching its neck and holding its head near the ground. He now knew the origin of the sound which had—no, not frightened him (of course not!), but slightly surprised him the evening before.

And, lo! there, immediately in front of him as he emerged, was the Edam Water, sliding and rippling on under its willows, the slim, silvery-grey leaves showing their white under-sides just as usual. There, across the river, were the cattle, standing already knee-deep in the shallows, their tails nervy and switchy on the alert for the morning's crop of flies. There was Mike going to drive them in to be milked. Yonder in the far distance was a black speck which must be Peter polishing straps and buckles hung on a pin by the stable door.

"Horrid beasts every one of them!" said Hugh John indignantly to himself, "going on all as comfortable as you please, just as if I had not been pining in a dungeon cell for years and years."

Then setting his cramped wet legs in motion, General Napoleon commenced a masterly retreat in the direction of home. He dashed for the stepping-stones, but he was in too much of a hurry to make sure of hitting them. He slipped from the first and went above the knee into the clear cool Edam Water. After that he simply floundered through, and presently emerged dripping on the other side. Along the woodland paths he scurried and scampered. He dashed across glades, scattering the rabbits and kicking up the dew in the joy of recovered freedom. He climbed a stone dyke into the home park, because he had no time to go round by the stile. He brought half of the fence down in his haste, scraping his knee as he did so. But so excited was he that he scarcely felt the additional bruise.

He ran up the steps. The front door was standing wide open, with the disreputable and tell-tale air of a reveller who has been out all night in evening dress. All doors have this look which have not been decently shut and locked during the dark hours. There was no one in the hall—no one in the dining-room—no one in the schoolroom, where the children's tea of the night before had never been cleared away. Hugh John noticed that his own place had been set, and the clean cup and plate and the burnished unused knife struck him as infinitely pathetic.

But he was hungry, and had no time to waste on mere feelings. His inner man was too insistent. He knew well where the pantry was (trust him for that!), and he went towards it at the rate of twenty miles an hour. He wished he had remembered to add a petition to his prayer that it might be unlocked. But it was now too late for this, so he must just trust in an unjogged Providence and take his chances.

The gods were favourable. They had evidently agreed that for one small boy he had suffered enough for that day. The pantry was unlocked. There was a lovely beefsteak pie standing on a shelf. Hugh John lifted it off, set it on the candle box, ungratefully throwing Sambo Soulis on the floor in order to make elbow room, and then with a knife and fork he proceeded to demolish the pie. The knife and fork he first put his hands on had obviously been used. But did General Napoleon stop to go to the schoolroom for clean ones? No—several thousand times no! Those who can, for a single moment, entertain such thoughts, are very far from having yet made the acquaintance of General Smith. Why, he did not even wait to say grace—though he usually repeated half-a-dozen the first thing in the morning, so as to have the job well over for the day. It is all right to say grace, but it is such a fag to have to remember before every meal. So Hugh John went into the wholesale business.

He was half through the pie before he looked about for something to drink. Lemonade, if it could be found, would meet the case. Hugh John felt this keenly, and, lo! the friendly Fates, with a smile, had planted a whole case of it at his feet. He knocked in the patent stopper with the handle of his knife (all things must yield to military necessity), and, after the first draught, what more was there left to live for—except a second bottle and the rest of the pie?

He was just doing his best to live up to the nice cool jelly, which melted in a kind of lingering chill of delight down his throat, when Janet Sheepshanks appeared in the doorway. Wearily and disheartenedly, she had come in to prepare for a breakfast which no one in all Windy Standard would eat. Something curious about the feeling of the house had struck her as she entered. She had gone from room to room, divided between hope and apprehension, and, lo! there before her, in her own ravished pantry, tuck-full of beefsteak pie and lemonade, sat the boy for whom they were even then dragging the deepest pools of the Edam.

"Oh, thank the Lord, laddie!" cried Janet, clasping her hands in devout thankfulness, "that He hath spared ye to your widowed faither—and to me, your auld unworthy nurse!"

The tears were running down her cheeks. Somehow her face had quite suddenly grown grey and worn. She looked years older than she had done yesterday. Hugh John paused and looked at her marvelling. He had a heavily laden fork half-way to his mouth. He wondered what all the fuss was about.

"Do get me some mustard, Janet," he said, swinging his wet legs; "and where on earth have you put the pickles?"

In the cross-examination which naturally followed, Hugh John kept his own counsel, like the prudent warrior he was. He left Janet and the others to suppose that, in trying to escape from his foes, he had "fallen" into the castle dungeon, and none of the household servants knew enough of the topography of the ancient stronghold to know that, if he had done so, he would probably have broken his neck. He said nothing about Nipper Donnan or any of the band by name. Simply and truthfully he designated them as "some bad boys," which certainly was in no way overstating the case.

Perhaps if his father had been at home he could not have hoodwinked his questioners so easily and completely. Mr. Picton Smith would certainly have gone deeper into the business than Janet Sheepshanks, who alternately slapped and scolded, petted and spoilt our hero all day long.

For some time Hugh John smelt of Araby the Blest and Spicy Ind; for he had ointments and liniments, rags and plasters innumerable scattered over his person in all directions.

He borrowed a cigarette (it was a very old and dry one) from the mantelpiece of his father's workroom, and retired to the shelter of the elm-tree to hold his court and take private evidence upon the events of yesterday.

As he went across the yard Black Donald ran bleating to him, and playfully butted at his leg.

Hugh John stopped in astonishment.

"Who found him?" he asked.

Sir Toady Lion proudly stepped forward. He had a garden rake in his hand, with which the moment before he had been poking Donald in the ribs, and making his life a burden to him generally.

"I CREATE YOU GENERAL OF THE COMM'SARIAT."

He began to speak, but Hugh John stopped him.

"Salute, you little beast!" he said sternly.

Slowly Toady Lion's hand went up. He did not object to salute, but he had a vague sense that, as a matter of personal dignity, not even a general had a right to speak to a private thus—much less to a commissariat sergeant. However, what he had to say was so triumphant and overpowering that he waived the point and touched his forehead in due form.

"I did—nobody but me. I d'livered him, all by mineself. I cutted the rope and d'livered Donald. Yes, I did—Prissy will tell 'oo. I wented into the Black Sheds all alone-y—and d'livered him!"

His words came tumbling over each other in his haste. But he laid strong emphasis upon the word "delivered," which he had just learned from Prissy. He meant to use it very often all that day, because it was a good word, and nobody knew the meaning of it except Quite-Grown-Ups.

General Napoleon Smith put on his most field-marshalish expression, and summoned Sir Toady Lion to approach.

He tapped him on the shoulder and said in a grand voice, "I create you General of the Comm'sariat for distinguished conduct in the field. From this time forth you can keep the key of the biscuit box, but I know just how many are in. So mind out!"

This was good, and Toady Lion was duly grateful; but he wished his good fortune put into a more concrete form.

"Can I have the biggest and nicerest saucer of the scrapings of the preserving-pan to-night?"

Hugh John considered a moment. An impulse of generosity swept over him.

"Yes, you can," he said nobly. Then a cross wave of caution caused him to add—"that is, if it isn't rasps!"

Now the children of the house of Windy Standard were permitted to clean out the boiling-pan in the fruit-preserving season with worn horn spoons, in order not to scratch the copper or crack the enamel. And rasp was Hugh John's favourite.

"Huh," said Toady Lion, turning up a contemptuous nose. "Thank 'oo for nuffin! I like wasps just as much as 'oo, Hugh John Picton Smiff!"

"Don't answer me back, sir!"—Hugh John was using his father's words and manner.

"Sall if I like," said Toady Lion, beginning to whimper. "Sall go and tell Janet Sheepshanks, and she'll give me yots of wasps! Not scrapin's neither, but weal-weal wasps—so there!"

"Toady Lion, I shall degrade you to the ranks. You are a little pig and a disgrace to the army."

"Don't care, I wants wasps—and I d'livered Donald," reiterated the Disgrace of the Army.

Hugh John once more felt the difficulty of arguing with Toady Lion. He was altogether too young to be logical. So he said, "Toady Lion, you little ass, stop snivelling—and I'll give you a bone button and the half of a knife."

"Let's see them," said Toady Lion, cautiously uncovering one eye by lifting up the edge of the covering palm. His commanding officer produced the articles of peace, and Toady Lion examined them carefully, still with one eye. They proved satisfactory.

"All yight!" said he, "I won't cry no more—but I wants three saucers full of the wasps too!"

CHAPTER XXII

MUTINY IN THE CAMP.

HUGH John was holding his court under the weeping-elm, and was being visited in detail by his army. The Carters had come over, and, after a vigorous engagement and pursuit, he had even forgiven Sammy for his lack of hardihood in not resisting to the death at the great battle of the Black Sheds.

"But it hurts so confoundedly," argued Sammy; "if it didn't, I shouldn't mind getting killed a bit!"

"Look at me," said Hugh John; "I'm all over peels and I don't complain."

"Oh! I dare say—it's all very well for you," retorted Sammy, "you like to fight, and it was you that began the fuss, but I only fight because you'd jolly-well-hammer me if I didn't!"

"Course I would," agreed his officer, "don't you know that's what generals are for?"

"Well," concluded Sammy Carter, summing the matter up philosophically, "'tain't my castle anyway."

The review was over. In the safe quiet of the elm-tree shelter General Napoleon might have been seen taking his well-earned repose. He was surrounded by his entire following—except, of course, the two Generals of Division, who were engaged in sweeping out the stable-yard. But these were considered socially supernumerary at any rate, except (a somewhat important exception) when there was fighting to be done.

"I don't see that we've done so very much to make a brag about anyhow," began Sammy Carter.

General Smith dexterously caught him on the ear with a young turnip, which in company with several friends had wandered in of its own accord from the nearest field on the home farm.

"I should say you didn't do much!" he sneered pointedly; "you hooked it as hard as you could after the first skirmish. Why, you haven't got a single sore place about you to show for it."

"Yes, I have!" retorted Sammy in high indignation.

"SAMMY CARTER MUTINOUS."

"Well, let's see it then!" commanded his general in a kindlier tone.

"Can't—ladies present!" said Sammy succinctly, into the retreating rear-guard of whose division the triumphant enemy had charged with the pike snatched from his sister's hands.

"All my wounds are in front. I fought and died with my face to the foe!" said Hugh John in his noblest manner.

"And I d'livered Donald!" contributed Toady Lion complacently.

"Oh, that ain't anything," sneered Sammy Carter, who was not in a good humour. His tone roused General Napoleon, who had the strong family feelings of all the Buonapartes.

"Shut up, Sammy, or I'll come and kick you. None of us did anything except Toady Lion. You ran away, and I got taken prisoner. Toady Lion is the only man among us!"

"I runned away too—at first," confessed the candid Toady Lion, who felt that he had so much real credit that he did not need to take a grain more than he deserved. "But I comed back quick—and I d'livered Donald out of prison, anyway—I did!"

Sammy Carter evidently had a sharp retort ready on the tip of his tongue, but he knew well the price he would have to pay for uttering it. Hugh John's eye was upon him, his right hand was closing on a bigger turnip—so Sammy forbore. But he kicked his feet more discontentedly than ever into the turf.

"Well," he said, changing the venue of the argument, "I don't think much of your old castle anyway. My father could have twice as good a castle if he liked——"

"Oh, 'course he could"—Hugh John's voice was distinctly ironical—"he might plant it on a peaty soil, and grow it from seed in two years; or perhaps he would like a cutting off ours!"

Mr. Davenant Carter was a distinguished agriculturist and florist.

"Don't you speak against my father!" cried Sammy Carter, glowering at General Napoleon in a way in which privates do not often look at their Commanders-in-Chief.

"Who's touching your father?" the latter said, a little more soothingly. "See here, Sammy, you've got your coat on wrong side out to-day. Go home and sleep on it. 'Tisn't my fault if you did run away, and got home before your sister—with a blue place on your back."

Sammy Carter flung out from under the shelter of the elm and went in search of Prissy, from whom in all his moods he was sure of comfort and understanding. He was a somewhat delicate boy, and generally speaking hated quarrelling as much as she did; but he had a clever tongue, which often brought him into trouble, and, like most other humorists, he did not at all relish a jest at his own expense.

As he went, he was pursued and stung by the brutally unrefined taunts of Hugh John.

"Yes, go on to Prissy; I think she has a spare doll. Go and play at 'house'! It's all you're good for!"

Thus encouraged by their general, the rest of the company—that is, Cissy and Sir Toady Lion, joined in singing a certain stirring and irritating refrain popular among the youth of Bordershire.

"Lassie-boy, lassie-boy, fie for shame! Coward's your nature, and Jennie's your name!"

Sammy Carter stood poised for flight with his eyes blazing with anger.

"You think a lot of your old tumble-down castle; but the town boys have got it in spite of you; and what's more, they've a flag flying on it with 'Down with Smith!' on it. I saw it. Hooray for the town boys!"

And with this Parthian arrow he disappeared at full speed down the avenue.

For a moment Hugh John was paralysed. He tried to pooh-pooh the matter, but he could not but admit that it might very well be true; so he instantly despatched Toady Lion for Prissy, who, as we know, was the fleetest runner of them all. Upon her reporting for duty, the General sent her to bring back word if the state of affairs was as reported.

It was. A large red flag was flying, with the inscription in white upon it, "Down with Smith!" while above the inscription there was what looked like a rude attempt at a death's head and crossbones. Hugh John knew this ensign in a moment. Once upon a time, in his wild youth, he had served under it as a pirate on the high seas; but of this he now uttered no word.

It was in such moments that the true qualities of the born leader came out in General Napoleon Smith. Instantly he dismissed his attendants, put his finger to his forehead, and sat down to draw a map of the campaign in the genuine Napoleonic manner.

At last, after quite a while, he rapped upon the table.

"I have it," he cried, "we must find an ally." The problem was solved.

CHAPTER XXIII

CISSY CARTER, BOYS' GIRL.

NOW Prissy Smith was a girls' girl, while Cissy Carter was a boys' girl. That was mainly the difference between them. Not that Prissy did not love boys' play upon occasion, for which indeed her fleetness of foot particularly fitted her. Also if Hugh John teased her she never cried nor told on him, but waited till he was looking the other way and then gave him something for himself on the ear. But on the whole she was a girls' girl, and her idea of the way to fight was slapping her dolls when they were naughty.

Now, Mr. Picton Smith said that most religion was summed up in two maxims, "Don't tell lies," and "Don't tell tales." To these Hugh John added a third, at least equal in canonicity, "Don't be dasht-mean." In these you have briefly comprehended all the Law and the Prophets of the house of Windy Standard.

Cissy Carter, however, was a tom-boy: you could not get over that. There was no other word for her. She never played with girls if she could better herself. She despised dolls; she hated botany and the piano. Her governess had a hard but lively time of it, and had it not been for her brother Sammy coaching her in short cuts to knowledge, she would have been left far behind in the exact sciences of spelling and the multiplication-table. As it was, between a tendency to scramble for scraps of information and the run of a pretty wide library, Cissy knew more than any one gave her credit for.

On one memorable occasion it was Cissy's duty to take her grandmother for a walk. Now the Dowager Mrs. Davenant Carter was the dearest and most fairy-like old lady in the world, and Cissy was very proud to walk into Edam with her. For her grandmother had not forgotten how good confections tasted to girls of thirteen, and there was quite a nice shop in the High Street. Their rose-drops especially were almost as good as doing-what-you-were-told-not-to, and their peppermints for use in church had quite the force of a religious observance.

But Mrs. Davenant Carter had a weak eye, and whenever she went out, she put a large green shade over it. So one day it happened that Cissy was walking abroad with her grandmother, with a vision of rose-drop-shop in the offing. As they were passing one of the villas nearest to their house, a certain rude boy, Wedgwood Baker the name of him, seeing the lame old lady tripping by on her stick like a fairy godmother, called out loudly "Go it, old blind patch!"

He was sorry the minute after, for in one moment Cissy Carter had pulled off her white thread gloves, climbed the fence, and had landed what Hugh John would have called "One, two, three—and a tiger" upon the person of Master Wedgwood Baker.

I do not say that all Cissy Carter's blows were strictly according to Queensberry rules. But at any rate the ungallant youth was promptly doubled up, and retreated yelling into the house, as it were falling back upon his reserves.

That same evening the card of Mrs. Baker, Laurel Villa, Edam, was brought to the diningtable of Mrs. Davenant Carter.

"The lady declines to come in, m'am. She says she must see you immediately at the door," said the scandalised housemaid.

Cissy's mother went into the hall with the card in her hand, and a look of gentle surprised inquiry on her face. There, on the doorstep was Mrs. Baker, with a young and hopeful but sadly damaged Wedgwood tagging behind her, like a weak-minded punt in tow of an ancient threedecker.

"'LOOK AT HIM, MADAM,' SAID MRS. BAKER."

The injured lady began at once a voluble complaint.

"Look at him, madam. That is the handiwork of your daughter. The poor boy was quietly digging in the garden, cultivating a few unpretending flowers, when your daughter, madam, suddenly flew at him over the railings and struck him on the face so furiously that, if I had not come to the rescue, the dear boy might have lost the use of both his eyes. But most happily I heard the disturbance and went out and stopped her."

"Dear me, this is very sad," faltered little Mrs. Carter; "I'm sure I don't know what can have come over Cissy. Are you sure there is no mistake?"

"Mistake! No, indeed, madam, there is no mistake, I saw her with my own eyes—a great girl twice Wedgwood's size."

At this point Mr. Davenant Carter came to the door with his table-napkin in his hand.

"What's this—what's this?" he demanded in his quick way—"Cissy and your son been fighting?"

"No indeed, sir," said the complainant indignantly; "this dear boy never so much as lifted a hand to her. Ah, here she comes—the very—ahem, young lady herself."

All ignorant of the trouble in store for her, Cissy came whistling through the laurels with half-a-dozen dogs at her heels. At sight of her Mrs. Baker bridled and perked her chin with indignation till all her black bugles clashed and twinkled.

"Come here, Cissy," said her father sternly. "Did you strike this boy to-day in front of his mother's gate?"

"Yes, I did," quoth the undaunted Cissy, "and what's more, I'll do it again, and give him twice as much, if he ever dares to call my grandmother 'Old Blind Patch' again—I don't care if he is two years and three months older than me!"

"Did you call names at my mother?" demanded Cissy's father, towering up very big, and looking remarkably stern.

Master Wedgwood had no denial ready; but he had his best boots on and he looked very hard at them.

"Come, Wedgwood dear, tell them that you did not call names. You know you could not!"

"I never called nobody names. It was her that hit me!" snivelled Wedgwood.

"Now, you hear," said his mother, as if that settled the question.

"Oh, you little liar! Wait till I catch you out!" said Cissy, going a step nearer as if she would like to begin again. "I'll teach you to tell lies on me."

Mrs. Baker of Laurel Villa held up her hands so that the lace mitts came together like the fingers of a figure of grief upon a tomb. "What a dreadful girl!" she said, looking up as if to ask

Heaven to support her.

Mr. Davenant Carter remembered his position as a county magistrate. Also he desired to stand well with all his neighbours.

"Madam," he said to Mrs. Baker, in the impressive tone in which he addressed public meetings, "I regret exceedingly that you should have been put to this trouble. I think that for the future you will have no reason to complain of my daughter. Will you allow me to conduct you across the policies by the shorter way? Cissy, go to bed at once, and stop there till I bid you get up! That will teach you to take the law into you own hands when your father is a Justice of the Peace!"

This he said in such a stern voice that Mrs. Baker was much flattered and quite appeased. He walked with the lady to the small gate in the boundary wall, opened it with his private key, and last of all shook hands with his visitor with the most distinguished courtesy. Some day he meant to stand for the burgh and her brothers were well-to-do grocers in the town.

"Sir," she said in parting, "I hope you will not be too severe with the young lady. Perhaps after all she was only a trifle impulsive!"

"Discipline must be maintained," said Mr. Davenant Carter sternly, closing, however, at the same time the eyelid most remote from Mrs. Baker of Laurel Villa.

"It shows what a humbug pa is," muttered Cissy, as she went upstairs; "he knows very well it is bed-time anyway. I don't believe he is angry one bit!"

When her father came in, he looked over at his wife. I am afraid he deliberately winked, though in the interests of morality I trust I may be mistaken. For how could a Justice of the Peace and a future Member of Parliament demean himself to wink?

"Jane," he said to Mrs. Carter, "what does Cissy like most of all for supper?"

"A little bit of chicken and bread-sauce done with broiled bacon—at least I think so, dear—why do you ask?"

He called the tablemaid.

"Walbridge," he said sternly, "take that disgraceful girl up the breast and both wings of a chicken, also three nice pieces of crisp bacon, four new potatoes with butter-sauce, some raspberrytart with thick cream and plenty of sugar—and a whole bottle of zoedone. But mind you, nothing else, as you value your place—not another bite for such a bold bad girl. This will teach her to go about the country thrashing boys two years older than herself!"

He looked over across the table at his son.

"Let this be a lesson to you, sir," he said, frowning sternly at him.

"Yes, sir," said Sammy meekly, winking in his turn very confidentially at a fly which was having a free wash and brush-up on the edge of the fingerbowl, after completing the round of the dishes on the dinner table.

CHAPTER XXIV

CHARITY BEGINS AT HOME—AND ENDS THERE.

NOW all this has nothing to do with the story, except to show what sort of a girl Cissy Carter was, and how she differed from Prissy Smith—who in these circumstances would certainly have gone home and prayed that God would in time make Wedgwood Baker a better boy, instead of tackling missionary work on the spot with her knuckles as Cissy Carter did.

It was several days later, and the flag of the Smoutchy boys still flew defiantly over the battlements of the castle. The great General was growing discouraged, for in little more than a week his father might return from London, and would doubtless take up the matter himself. Then, with the coming of policemen and the putting up of fences and notice-boards, all romance would be gone forever. Besides which, most of the town boys would have to go back to school, and the Carters' governess and their own would be returning to annoy them with lessons, and still more uncalled for aggravations as to manners.

Cissy Carter had given Sammy the slip, and started to come over by herself to Windy Standard. It was the afternoon, and she came past the gipsy encampment which Mr. Picton Smith had found on some unenclosed land on the other side of the Edam Water, and which, spite of the remonstrances of his brother-landlords, he had permitted to remain there.

The permanent Ishmaelitish establishment consisted of about a dozen small huts, some entirely constructed of rough stone, others of turf with only a stone interposed here and there; but all had mud chimneys, rough doorways, and windows glazed with the most extraordinary collection of old glass, rags, wisps of straw, and oiled cloth. Dogs barked hoarsely and shrilly according to their kind, ragged clothes fluttered on extemporised lines, or made a parti-coloured patch-work on the grass and on the gorse bushes which grew all along the bank. There were also a score of tents and caravans dotted here and there about the rough ground. Half-a-dozen swarthy lads rose silently and stared after Cissy as she passed.

A tall limber youth sitting on a heap of stones examining a dog's back, looked up and scowled as she came by. Cissy saw an unhealed wound and stopped.

"Let me look at him," she said, reaching out her hand for the white fox-terrier.

"Watch out, miss," said the lad, "he's nasty with the sore. He'll bite quick as mustard!"

"He won't bite me," said Cissy, taking up the dog calmly, which after a doubtful sniff submitted to be handled without a murmur.

"This should be thoroughly washed, and have some boracic ointment put on it at once," said Cissy, with the quick emphasis of an expert.

"Ain't got none o' the stuff," said the youth sullenly, "nor can't afford to buy it. Besides, who's to wash him first off, and him in a temper like that?"

"Come over with me to Oaklands and I'll get you some ointment. I'll wash him myself in a minute."

The boy whistled.

"That's a good 'un," he said, "likely thing me to go to Oaklands!"

"And why?" said Cissy; "it's my father's place. I've just come from there."

"Then your father's a beak, and I ain't going a foot—not if I know it," said the lad.

"A what—oh! you mean a magistrate—so he is. Well, then, if you feel like that about it I'll run over by myself, and sneak some ointment from the stables."

And with a careless wave of the hand, a pat on the head and a "Poo' fellow then" to the white fox-terrier, she was off.

The youth cast his voice over his shoulders to a dozen companions who were hiding in the broom behind. His face and tone were both full of surprise and admiration.

"'LET ME LOOK AT HIM,' SHE SAID."

"Say, chaps, did you hear her? She said shc'd 'sneak' the ointment from the stables. I tell 'ee what, she'll be a rare good plucked one that. And her a beak's daughter! Her mother mun ha' been a piece!"

It was half-an-hour before Cissy got back with the pot of boracic dressing and some lint.

"I had to wait till the coachman had gone to his tea," she explained, "and then send the stable boy with a message to the village to get him out of the way."

The youth on the stone heap secretly signalled his delight to the appreciative audience hiding in the broom bushes.

Then Cissy ordered him to get her some warm water, which he brought from one of the kettles swinging on the birchen tripods scattered here and there about the encampment.

Whereupon, taking the fox-terrier firmly on her knee and turning up the skirt of her dress, she washed away all the dirt and matted hair, cleansing the wound thoroughly.

The poor beast only made a faint whining sound at intervals. Then she applied the antiseptic dressing, and bound the lint tightly down with a cincture about the animal. She fitted his neck with a neat collar of her own invention, made out of the wicker covering of a Chianti wine flask which she brought with her from Oaklands.

"There," she said, "that will keep him from biting at it, and you must see that he doesn't scratch off the bandage. I'll be passing to-morrow and will drop in. Here's the pot of ointment. Put some more on in the morning and some again at night, and he will be all right in a day or two."

"Thank'ee, miss," said the lad, touching his cap with the natural courtesy which is inherent in the best blood of his race. "I don't mean to forget, you be sure."

Cissy waved her hand to him gaily, as she went off towards Windy Standard. Then all at once she stopped.

"By the way, what is your name? Whom shall I ask for if you are not about to-morrow?"

"Billy Blythe," he said, after a moment's pause to consider whether the daughter of a magistrate was to be trusted; "but I'll be here to-morrow right enough!"

"Why did you tell the beak's daughter your name, Bill, you blooming Johnny?" asked a companion. "You'll get thirty days for that sure!"

"Shut up, Fish Lee," said the owner of the dog; "the girl is main right. D'ye think she'd ha' said 'sneaked' if she wasn't. G'way, Bacon-chump!"

Cissy Carter took the road to Windy Standard with a good conscience. She was not troubled about the "sneaking," though she hoped that the coachman would not miss that pot of ointment.

At the foot of the avenue, just where it joined the dusty road to the town of Edam, she met Sir Toady Lion. He had his arms full of valuable sparkling jewellery, or what in the distance looked like it as the sun shone upon some winking yellow metal.

Toady Lion began talking twenty to the dozen as soon as ever he came within Cissy's range.

"Oo!" he cried, "what 'oo fink? Father sented us each a great big half-crown from London—all to spend. And we have spended it."

"Well," said Cissy genially, "and what did you buy?"

"Us all wented down to Edam and boughted—oh! yots of fings."

"Show me what you've bought, Toady Lion! I want to see! How much money had you, did you say?"

Toady Lion sat plump down in the thickest dust of the road, as he always did just wherever he happened to be at the time. If there chanced to be a pool there or a flower-bed—why, so much the worse. But whenever Toady Lion wanted to sit down, he sat down. Here, however, there was only the dry dust of the road and a brown smatter of last year's leaves. The gallant knight was in a meditative mood and inclined to moralise.

"Money," said Toady Lion thoughtfully, "well, dere's the money that you get gived you, and wot Janet sez you muss put in your money-box. That's no good! Money-box locked! Janet keeps money-box. 'Get money when you are big,' she sez—rubbage, I fink—shan't want it then—lots and lots in trowsies' pocket then, gold sixpences and fings."

Toady Lion's eyes were dreamy and glorious, as if the angels were whispering to him, and he saw unspeakable things,

"Then there's miss'nary money in a round box wif a slit on the top. That's lots better! Sits on mantlepiece in dining-room. Can get it out wif slimmy-jimmy knife when nobody's looking. Hugh John showed me how. Prissy says boys who grab miss'nary's pennies won't not go to heaven, but Hugh John, he says—yes. 'Cause why miss'nary's money is for bad wicked people to make them good. Then if it is wicked to take miss'nary money, the money muss be meaned for us—to do good to me and Hugh John. Hugh John finks so. Me too!"

Toady Lion spoke in short sentences with pauses between, Cissy meantime nodding appreciation.

"Yes, I know," she said meditatively, "a thinbladed kitchen knife is best."

But Sir Toady Lion had started out on the track of Right and Wrong, and was intent on running them down with his usual slow persistence.

"And then the miss'nary money is weally-weally our money, 'cause Janet makes us put it in. Onst Hugh John tried metal buttons off of his old serge trowsies. But Janet she found out. And he got smacked. An' nen, us only takes a penny out when us is tony-bloke!"

"Is which? Oh, stone-broke," laughed Cissy Carter, sitting down beside Toady Lion; "who taught you to say that word?"

"Hugh John," said the small boy wistfully; "him and me tony-bloke all-ee-time, all-ee-ways, all-ee-while!"

"Does Prissy have any of—the missionary money?" said Cissy; "I should!"

"No," said Toady Lion sadly; "don't you know? Our Prissy's awful good, juss howwid! She likes goin' to church, an' washing, an' having to wear gloves. Girls is awful funny."

"They are," said Cissy Carter promptly. The funniness of her sex had often troubled her. "But tell me, Toady Lion," she went on, "does Hugh John like going to church, and being washed, and things?"

"Who? Hugh John—him?" said Toady Lion, with slow contempt. "'Course he don't. Why, he's a boy. And once he told Mr. Burnham so—he did."

Mr. Burnham was the clergyman of both families. He had recently come to the place, was a well-set up bachelor, and represented a communion which was not by any means the dominant one in Bordershire.

"Yes, indeedy. It was under the elm. Us was having tea. An' Mist'r Burnham, he was having tea. And father and Prissy. And, oh! such a lot of peoples. And he sez, Mist'r Burnham sez to Hugh John, 'You are good little boy. I saw you in church on Sunday. Do you like to go to church?' He spoke like this-a-way, juss like I'm tellin' oo, down here under his silk waistcoat—kind of growly, but nice."

"Hugh John say that he liked to go to church—'cos father was there listenin', you see. Then Mist'r Burnham ask Hugh John why he like to go to church, and of course, he say wight out that it was to look at Sergeant Steel's wed coat. An' nen everybody laugh—I don't know why. But Mist'r Burnham he laughed most."

Cissy also failed to understand why everybody should have laughed. Toady Lion took up the burden of his tale.

"Yes, indeedy, and one Sunday I didn't have to go to church—'cos I'd yet up such a yot of gween gooseb——"

"All right, Toady Lion, I know!" interrupted Cissy quickly.

"Of gween gooseberries," persisted Toady Lion calmly; "so I had got my tummy on in front. It hurted like—well, like when you get sand down 'oo trowsies. Did 'oo ever get sand in 'oo trowsies, Cissy?"

"Hush—of course not!" said Cissy Carter; "girls don't have trowsers—they have——"

But any injudicious revelations on Cissy's part were stopped by Toady Lion, who said, "No, should juss fink not. Girls is too great softs to have trowsies.

"Onst though on the sands at a seaside, when I was 'kye-kying' out loud an' kickin' fings, 'cos I was not naughty but only fractious, dere was a lady wat said 'Be dood, little boy, why can't you be dood?'

"An' nen I says, 'How can I be dood? Could 'oo be dood wif all that sand in 'oo trowsies?'

"An' nen—the lady she wented away quick, so quick—I can't tell why. P'raps she had sand in her trowsies! Does 'oo fink so, Cissy?"

"That'll do—I quite understand," said Cissy Carter, somewhat hastily, in dread of Toady Lion's well-known license of speech.

"An' nen 'nother day after we comed home I went into the park and clum up a nice tree. An' it was ever so gween and scratchy. 'An it was nice. Nen father he came walking his horse slow up the road, n' I hid. But father he seen me. And he say, 'What you doing there, little boy? You break you neck. Nen I whip you. Come down, you waskal!' He said it big—down here, (Toady Lion illustrated with his hand the place from which he supposed his father's voice to proceed). An' it made me feel all queer an' trimbly, like our guinea pig's nose when father speak like that. An' I says to him, 'Course, father, you never clumb up no trees on Sundays when you was little boy!' An' nen he didn't speak no more down here that trimbly way, but laughed, and pulled me down, and roded me home in front of him, and gived me big hunk of pie—yes, indeedy!"

Toady Lion felt that now he had talked quite enough, and began to arrange his brass cannons on the dust, in a plan of attack which beleaguered Cissy Carter's foot and turned her flank to the left.

"Where did you get all those nice new cannons? You haven't told me yet," she said.

"Boughted them!" answered Toady Lion promptly, "least I boughted some, and Hugh John boughted some, an' Prissy she boughted some."

"And how do you come to have them all?" asked Cissy, watching the imposing array. As usual it was the Battle of Bannockburn and the English were getting it hot.

"Well," said Toady Lion thoughtfully, "'twas this way. 'Oo sees Prissy had half-a-crown, an' she boughted a silly book all about a 'Lamplighter' for herself—an' two brass cannons—one for Hugh John an' one for me. And Hugh John he had half-a-crown, an' he boughted three brass cannon, two for himself and one for me."

"And what did you buy with your half-crown?" said Cissy, bending her brows sweetly upon the small gunner.

"Wif my half-a-crown? Oh, I just boughted three brass cannons—dey was all for mine-self!"

"Toady Lion," cried Cissy indignantly, "you are a selfish little pig! I shan't stop with you any more."

"Little pigs is nice," said Toady Lion, unmoved, arranging his cannon all over again on a new plan after the removal of Cissy's foot; "their noses——"

"Don't speak to me about their noses, you selfish little boy! Blow your own nose."

"No use," said Toady Lion philosophically; "won't stay blowed. 'Tis too duicy!"

Cissy set off in disgust towards the house of Windy Standard, leaving Toady Lion calmly playing with his six cannon all alone in the white dust of the king's highway.

CHAPTER XXV

LOVE'S (VERY) YOUNG DREAM.

CISSY found our hero in a sad state of depression. Prissy had gone off to evening service, and had promised to introduce a special petition that he might beat the Smoutchy boys; but Gen'l Smith shook his head.

"With Prissy you can't never tell. Like as not she may go and pray that Nipper Donnan may get converted, or die and go to heaven, or something like that. She'd do it like winking, without a thought for how I should feel! That's the sort of girl our Priss is!"

"Oh, surely not so bad as that," said Cissy, very properly scandalised.

"She would, indeed," said Hugh John, nodding his head vehemently; "she's good no end, our Prissy is. And never shirks prayers, nor forgets altogether, nor even says them in bed. I believe she'd get up on a frosty night and say them without a fire—she would, I'm telling you. And she doats on these nasty Smoutchies. She'd just love to have been tortured. She'd have regularly spread herself on forgiving them too, our Priss would."

"I wouldn't have forgiven them," cried the piping voice of Toady Lion, suddenly appearing through the shrubbery (his own more excellent form was "scrubbery"), with his arms full of the new brass cannons; "I wouldn't have forgiven them a bit. I'd have cutted off all their heads."

"Go 'way, little pig!" cried Cissy indignantly.

"Toady Lion isn't a little pig," said Hugh John, with dignity; "he is my brother."

"But he kept all the cannons to himself," remonstrated Cissy.

"'Course he did; why shouldn't he? He's only a little boy, and can't grow good all at once," said Hugh John, with more Christian charity than might have been expected of him.

"You've been growing good yourself," said Cissy, thrusting out her upper lip with an expression of bitter reproach and disappointment; "I'd better go home."

"I'll hit you if you say that, Cissy," cried Hugh John, "but anyway you shan't call Toady Lion a little pig."

"I like being little pig," said Toady Lion impassively; "little piggie goes 'Grunt-grunt!'"

And he illustrated the peculiarities of piglings by pulling the air up through his nostrils in various keys. "Little pigs is nice," he repeated at the end of this performance.

Cissy was very angry. Things appeared to be particularly horrid that afternoon. She had started out to help everybody, and had only managed to quarrel with them. Even her own familiar Hugh John had lifted up his heel against her. It was the last straw. But she was resolved to not give in now.

"Good little boy"—she said tauntingly—"it is such a mother's pet! It will be good then, and go and ask Nipper's pardon, and send back Donald to make nice mutton pies; it shall then——!"

Hugh John made a rush at this point. There was a wild scurry of flight, and the gravel flew every way. Cissy was captured behind the stable, and Hugh John was about to administer punishment. His hand was doubled. It was drawn back.

"Yes," cried Cissy, "hit a girl! Any boy can beat you. But you can hit a girl! Hit hard, brave soldier!"

Hugh John's hand dropped as if struck by lightning.

"I never did!" he said; "I fought ten of them at once and never even cried when they—when they——"

And the erstwhile dauntless warrior showed unmistakable signs of being perilously near a descent into the vale of tears.

"When they what?" queried Cissy softly, suddenly beginning to be sorry.

"Well, when they tortured me," said Hugh John.

"'HIT HARD, BRAVE SOLDIER.'"

Cissy went up suddenly and kissed him. It was only a peck which reached land at the top corner of his ear; but it made Hugh John crimson hotly, and fend Cissy off with his elbow as if she had been a big boy about to strike.

"There, now," she said, "I've done it. I promised I would, and what's more, I'll say it out loud— 'I love you!' There! And if you don't mind and behave, I'll tell people. I will, now then. But all the same, I'm sorry I was a beast to you."

"Well, don't do it again," said Hugh John, somewhat mollified, slightly dropping the point of his defensive elbow. "Anybody might have seen you, and then what would they think?"

"All right," said Cissy soothingly, "I won't any more."

"Say 'Hope-you-may-die!'"

Cissy promptly hoped she might come to an early grave in the event of again betraying, even in private, the exuberance of her young affection.

"Now, Hugh John," said Cissy, when peace had been restored in this manner, and they were wandering amicably across the back meadow where they could not be seen from the house windows, taking alternate sucks at a stick of brown toffee with crumbs stuck firmly on it, the property of Cissy, "I've something to tell you. I've found the allies for you; and we can whop the Smoutchies and take the castle now—any time."

The eyes of General Napoleon Smith glistened.

"If that's true," he said, "you can kiss me again—no, not now," he added hastily, moving off a little, "but after, when it's all over, you know. There's a good place behind the barn. You can do it there if you like."

"Will you say 'I love you, Cissy'?"

But this was more than Hugh John had bargained for. He asked time for consideration.

"It won't be till the Smoutchy boys are beaten and the castle ours for good," pleaded Cissy.

Hugh John felt that it was a great price to pay, but after all he did want dreadfully to beat the Smoutchy boys.

"Well, I'll try," he said, "but you must say, 'Hope-you'll-die and double-die,' if you ever tell!"

Again Cissy took the required oath.

"Well?" said he expectantly, his mind altogether on the campaign.

Cissy told him all about the gipsy encampment and the history of the meeting with Billy Blythe. Hugh John nodded. Of course he knew all about that, but would they join? Were they not rather on the side of the Smoutchies? They looked as if they would be.

"Oh, you can't never tell a bit beforehand," said Cissy eagerly. "They just hate the town boys; and Bill Blythe says that Nipper Donnan's father said, that when the town got the castle they would soon clear the gipsies off your common—for that goes with the castle."

Hugh John nodded again more thoughtfully. There was certainly something in that. He had heard his father say as much to his lawyer when he himself was curled up on the sofa, pretending to read Froissart's "Chronicles," but really listening as hard as ever he could.

"You are a brick," he cried, "you are indeed, Cissy. Come on, let's go at once and see Billy Blythe."

And he took her hand. She held back a moment. They were safe behind the great ivy bush at the back of the stables.

"Couldn't you say it now?" she whispered, with a soft light in her eyes; "I wish you could. Try."

Hugh John's face darkened. He unshipped his elbow from his side to be ready for action.

"Well, I won't ask you till after," she said regretfully. "'Tain't fair, I know; but—" she looked at him again yet more wistfully, still holding him by the hand which had last passed over the mutual joint-stock candy-stick; "don't you think you could do the other—just once?"

"What other?" grumbled Hugh John, sulking. He felt that Cissy was taking an unfair advantage.

"Oh, you know," said Cissy, "what I did to you a little while ago."

"'Twasn't to be till after," urged our hero, half relenting. Like a woman, Cissy was quick to see her advantage.

"Just a little one to be going on with?" she pleaded.

Hugh John sighed. Girls were incomprehensible. Prissy liked church and being washed. Cissy, of whom he had more hopes, liked kissing.

"Well," he said, "goodness knows why you like it. I'm sure I don't and never shall. But—"

He ran to the corner and looked round into the stable-yard. All was quiet along the Potomac. He walked more sternly to the other corner, and glanced into the orchard. Peace reigned among the apple-trees. He came slowly and dejectedly back. In the inmost corner of the angle of the stable, and behind the thickest of the ivy bush, he straightened himself up and compressed his lips, as he had done when the Smoutchies were tying him up by the thumbs. He felt however that to beat Nipper Donnan he was ready to undergo anything—even this. No sacrifice was too great.

"All right," he said. "Come on, Cissy, and get it over—only don't be too long."

Cissy was thirteen, and tall for her age, but though fully a year younger, Hugh John was tall also, so that when she came joyously forward and put her hands on his shoulders, their eyes were exactly on a level.

"You needn't go shutting your eyes and holding your breath, as if it were medicine. 'Tisn't so very horrid," said Cissy, with her hands still on his shoulder.

"Go on!" said Hugh John in a muffled voice, nerving himself for the coming crisis.

Cissy's lips just touched his, rested a moment, and were gone.

Hugh John let out his breath with a sigh of relief like an explosion; then he stepped back, and promptly wiped off love's gage with the sleeve of his coat.

"Hold on," cried Cissy; "that isn't fair. You know it ain't!"

Hugh John knew it and submitted.

Cissy swept the tumbled hair from about her eyes. She had a very red spot on either cheek; but she had made up her mind, and was going through with it properly now.

"'WASN'T IT SPLENDID?'"

"Oh, I don't mind," she said; "I can easily do it over again—for keeps this time, mind!"

Then she kissed him once, twice, and three times. It was nicer than kissing Janet Sheepshanks, he thought; and as for Prissy—well, that was different too.

A little hammer thumped in his heart, and made it go "jumpetty-jump," as if it were lame, or out of breath, or had one leg shorter than the other. After all Ciss was the nicest girl there was, if she did behave stupidly and tiresomely about this. "Just once?" He would do it after all. It wasn't much to do—to give Cissy such a treat.

So he put his arms about her neck underneath her curls, pulled her close up to him, and kissed her. It felt funny, but rather nice. He did not remember doing that to any one since he was a little boy, and his mother used to come and say "Good-night" to him. Then he opened his arms and pushed Cissy away. They walked out through the orchard yards apart, as if they had just been introduced. Cissy's eyes were full of the happiness of love's achievement. As for Hugh John, he was crimson to the neck and felt infinitely degraded in his own estimation.

They came to the orchard wall, where there was a stile which led in the direction of Oaklands. Cissy ran up the rude steps, but paused on the top instead of going over. Hugh John was looking the other way. Somehow, do what he would, his eyes could not be brought to meet hers.

"Are you not coming?" she said coaxingly.

"No," he answered, gruffly enough; "to-morrow will do for Billy."

"Good-night," she said softly. Her voice was almost a whisper.

Hugh John grunted inarticulately.

"Look here!" she said, bending down till her eyes were on a level with his chin. He could not help glancing up once. There was a mischievous smile in them. It had never struck him before that Cissy was very pretty. But somehow now he was glad that she was. Prissy was nice-looking too—but, oh! quiet different. He continued to look at Cissy Carter standing with the stile between them.

"Wasn't it splendid!" she said, still keeping her shining eyes on his.

"Oh, middling," said Hugh John, and turning on his heel he went into the stable without even saying "Good-bye." Cissy watched him with a happy smile on her face. Love was her fetish—her Sambo Soulis—and she had worshipped long in secret. Till now she had let the worm concealment prey upon her cheek. True, it had not as yet affected her appetite nor kept her a moment awake.

But now all was different. Her heart sang, and the strangest thing was that all the landscape, the fields and woods, and everything seemed to be somehow painted in brighter colours. In fact, they looked just as they do when you bend down and look at them through between your legs. You know the way.

CHAPTER XXVI

AN IMPERIAL BIRTHDAY.

THE next day was General Napoleon Smith's birthday. Outwardly it looked much like other days. There were not, as there ought to have been, great, golden imperial capital N's all over the sky. Nature indeed was more than usually calm; but, to strike a balance, there was excitement enough and to spare in and about the house of Windy Standard. Very early, when it was not yet properly light, but only sort of misty white along the wet grass and streaky combed-out grey up above in the sky, Prissy waked Sir Toady Lion, who promptly rolled over to the back of his cot, and stuck his funny head right down between the wall and the edge of the wire mattress, so that only his legs and square sturdy back could be seen.

Toady Lion always preferred to sleep in the most curious positions. In winter he usually turned right round in bed till his head was far under the bed-clothes, and his fat, twinkly, pink toes reposed peacefully on the pillow. Nothing ever mattered to Toady Lion. He could breathe through his feet just as well as through his mouth, and (as we have seen) much better than through his nose. The attention of professors of physiology is called to this fact, which can be established upon the amplest evidence and the most unimpeachable testimony. In summer he generally rolled out of bed during the first half hour, and slept comfortably all the rest of the night on the floor.

"Get up, Toady Lion," said his sister softly, so as not to waken Hugh John; "it is the birthday."

"Ow don' care!" grumbled Toady Lion, turning over and over three or four times very fast till he had all the bed-clothes wrapped about him like a cocoon; "don' care wat it is. I'se goin' to sleep some more. Don't go 'prog' me like that!"

"Come," said Prissy gently, to tempt him; "we are going to give Hugh John a surprise, and sing a lovely hymn at his door. You can have my ivory Prayer-book——"

"For keeps?" asked Toady Lion, opening his eyes with his first gleam of interest.

"Oh, no, you know that was mother's, and father gave it to me to take care of. But you shall have it to hold in your hand while we are singing."

"Well, then, can I have the picture of the anzel Michael castin' out the baddy-baddy anzels and hittin' the Bad Black Man O-such-a-whack on the head?"

Prissy considered. The print was particularly dear to her heart, and she had spent a happy wet Saturday colouring it. But she did want to make the birthday hymn a success, and Toady Lion had undeniably a fine voice when he liked to use it—which was not often.

"All right," she said, "you can have my 'Michael and the Bad Angels,' but you are not to spoil it."

"Shan't play then," grumbled Toady Lion, who knew well the strength of his position, and was as troublesome as a prima donna when she knows her manager cannot do without her—"shan't sing, not unless 'Michael and the Bad Angels' is mine to spoil if I like."

"But you won't—will you, dear Toady Lion?" pleaded Prissy. "You'll keep it so nice and careful, and then next Saturday, when I have my week's money and you are poor, I'll buy it off you again."

"Shan't promise," said the Obstinate Brat—as Janet, happily inspired, had once called him after being worsted in an argument, "p'rhaps yes, and p'rhaps no."

"Come on then, Toady Lion," whispered Prissy, giving him a hand and deciding to trust to luck for the preservation of her precious print. Toady Lion was often much better than his word, and she knew from experience that by Saturday his financial embarrassments would certainly be such that no reasonable offer was likely to be refused.

Toady Lion rose, and taking his sister's hand they went into her room, carefully shutting the door after them. Here Prissy proceeded to equip Toady Lion in one of her own "nighties," very much against that chorister's will.

"You see, pink flannel pyjams are not proper to sing in church in," she whispered: "now—you must hold your hymn-book so, and look up at the roof when you sing—like the 'Child Samuel' on the nursery wall."

"Mine eyes don't goggle like his," said Toady Lion, who felt that Nature had not designed him for the part, and who was sleepy and cross anyway. Birthdays were no good—except his own.

It happened that Janet Sheepshanks was going downstairs early to set the maids to their morning work, and this is what she saw. At the closed door of Hugh John's chamber stood two quaint little figures, clad in lawny white, one tall and slim, the other short and chubby as a painted cherub on a ceiling. They had each white hymn-books reverently placed between their hands. Their eyes were raised heavenwards and their lips were red and parted with excitement.

The stern Scotswoman felt something suddenly strike her heart.

"Eh, sir," she said, telling the tale afterwards, "the lassie Priscilla was sae like her mither, my puir bairn that is noo singing psalms wi' the angels o' God, that I declare, my verra heart stood still, for I thocht that she had come back for yin o' the bairns. And, oh! I couldna pairt wi' ony o' them noo. It wad fairly break my heart. And there the twa young things stood at the door, but when they began to sing, I declare I juist slippit awa' doon to the closet and grat on the tap o' a cask o' paraffeen!"

And this is what Janet Sheepshanks heard them sing. It was not perhaps very appropriate, but it was one of the only two hymns of which Toady Lion knew the words; and I think even Mr. Charles Wesley, who wrote it, would not have objected if he had seen the angelic devotion on Prissy's face or the fraudulent cherub innocence shining from that of Sir Toady Lion.

"Now, mind, your eyes on the crack of the door above," whispered Prissy; "and when I count three under my breath—sing out for your very life."

Toady Lion nodded.

"One—two—three!" counted Prissy.

"Hark! the herald angels sing, Glory to the new-born King, Peace on earth and mercy mild,
God and sinners reconciled."

"What is 'weconciled'?" asked Toady Lion, who must always ask something on principle.

"Oh, never mind now," whispered Prissy hastily; "keep your eyes on the top crack of the door and open your mouth wide."

"Don't know no more!" said Toady Lion obstinately.

"Oh yes, you do," said Prissy, almost in tears; "go on. Sing La-La, if you don't, and we'll soon be at the chorus, and you know that anyway!"

Then the voice of Prissy escaped, soaring aloft in the early gloom, and if any human music can, reaching the Seventh Sphere itself, where, amid the harmonies of the universe, the Eternal Ear hearkens for the note of sinful human praise.

The sweet shrill pipe of Toady Lion accompanied her like a heavenly lute of infinite sweetness. It was at this point that Janet made off in the direction of the paraffin barrel.

"Joyful all ye nations rise, Join the triumph of the skies: Universal nature, say, 'Christ the Lord is risen to-day!'"

The door opened, and the head of Hugh John appeared, his hair all on end and his pyjama jacket open at the neck. He was hitching up the other division of the suit with one hand.

"'Tain't Christmas, what's the horrid row? Shut it!" growled he sleepily. Prissy made him the impatient sign of silence so well understood of children, and which means that the proceedings are not to be interrupted.

"Your birthday, silly!" she said; "chorus now!" And Hugh John himself, who knew the value of discipline, lined up and opened his mouth in the loud rejoicing refrain:—

"Hark! the herald angels sing, Glory to the newborn King!"

A slight noise behind made them turn round, and there the children beheld with indignation the whole body of the servants grouped together on the landing, most of them with their handkerchiefs to their eyes; while Jane Housemaid who had none, was sobbing undisguisedly with the tears rolling down her cheeks, and vainly endeavouring to express her opinion that "it was just beautiful—they was for all the world like little angels a-praisin' God, and—a-hoo! I can't help it, no more I can't! And their mother never to see them growed up—her bein' in her grave, the blessed lamb!"

"I don't see nuffin to kye for," said Toady Lion unsympathetically, trying to find pockets in Prissy's night-gown; "it was a nice sing-song!"

At this moment Janet Sheepshanks came on the scene. She had been crying more than anybody, but you would never have guessed it. And now, perhaps ashamed of her own emotion, she pretended great scandal and indignation at the unseemly and irregular spectacle, and drove the servants below to their morning tasks, being specially severe with Jane Housemaid, who, for some occult reason, found it as difficult to stop crying as it had been easy to begin—so that, as Hugh John said, "it was as good as a watering-can, and useful too, for it laid the dust on Jane's carpets ready for sweeping, ever so much better than tea-leaves."

CHAPTER XXVII

THE BANTAM CHICKENS.

WHEN Hugh John met Cissy Carter the first time after the incident of the stile, it was in the presence of the young lady's father and mother. Cissy smiled and shook hands with the most serene and chilling dignity; but Hugh John blushed, and wore on his countenance an expression of such deep and ingrained guilt and confusion, that, upon catching sight of him, Mr. Davenant Carter called out, in his jolly stand-before-the-fire-with-his-hands-in-his-pockets' manner, "Hillo, boy! what have you been up to—stealing apples, eh? Come! What is it? Out with it!"

Which, when you think of it, was not exactly fitted to make our hero any more self-possessed. Mr. Davenant Carter always considered children as a rather superior kind of puppy dogs, which were specially created to be condescended to and teased, in order to see what they would say and do. They might also be taught tricks—like monkeys and parrots, only not so clever.

"Oh, Davenant," said his wife, "do let the boy alone. Don't you see he is bashful before so many people?"

Now this was the last thing which ordinarily could be laid with justice to the charge of our hero; yet now he only mumbled and avoided everybody's eye, particularly Cissy's. But apparently that young lady had forgotten all about the ivy bush at the back of the stable, for she said quite loud out, so that all the room could hear her, "What a long time it is since we saw you at Oaklands, Hugh John—isn't it?" This sally added still more to Hugh John's confusion, and he could only fall back upon his favourite axiom (which he was to prove the truth of every day of his life as he grew older), that "girls are funny things."

Presently Cissy said, "Have you seen Sammy, mother; I wonder if he has fallen into the mill-dam. He went over there more than an hour ago to sail his new boat." Mild Mrs. Carter started up so violently that she upset all her sewing cotton and spools on the floor, to the delight of her wicked little pug, which instantly began pulling them about, shaking them, growling at them, and pretending they were rats that had been given him to worry.

"Oh, do you think so?—Run Cissy, run Hugh, and find him!" Whereat Cissy and Hugh John removed themselves. As soon as they were outside our hero found his tongue.

"How could you tell such a whopper? Of course he would not fall into the water like a baby!"

"Goos-ee gander," said Cissy briskly; "of course not! I knew that very well. But if I had not said something we should have had to stay there moping among all those Grown-Ups, and doing nothing but talking proper for hours and hours."

"But I thought you liked it, Cissy," said Hugh John, who did not know everything.

"Like it!" echoed Cissy; "I've got to do it. And if they dreamed I didn't like it, they'd think I hadn't proper manners, and make me stop just twice as long. Mother wants me to acquire a good society something-or-other, so that's why I've to stop and make tea, and pretend to like to talk to Mr. Burnham."

"Oh—him," said Hugh John; "he isn't half bad. And he's a ripping good wicket-keep!"

"I dare say," retorted Cissy, "that's all very well for you. He talks to you about cricket and W.

G.'s scores—I've heard him. But he speaks to me in that peeky far-away voice from the back of his throat, like he does in the service when he comes to the bit about 'young children'—and what do you think the Creature says?"

"I dunno," said Hugh John, with a world-weary air, as if the eccentricities of clergymen in silk waistcoats were among the things that no fellow could possibly find out.

"Well, he said that he hoped the time would soon come when a young lady of so much decision of character (that's me!) would be able to assist him in his district visiting."

"What's 'decision of character' when he's at home?" asked Hugh John flippantly.

"Oh, nothing—only one of the things parsons say. It doesn't mean anything—not in particular!" replied the widely informed Cissy. "But did you ever hear such rot?"

And for the first time her eyes met his with a quaintly questioning look, which somehow carried in it a reminiscence of the stile and the ivy bush. Cissy's eyes were never quite (Hugh John has admitted as much to me in a moment of confidence)—never quite the same after the incident of the orchard. On this occasion Hugh John instantly averted his own, and looked stolidly at the ground.

"Perhaps Mr. Burnham has heard that you went with medicine and stuff to the gipsy camp," he said after a pause, trying to find an explanation of the apparently indefensible folly of his cricketing hero. Cissy had not thought of this before.

"Well, perhaps he had," she said, "but that was quite different."

"How different?" queried Hugh John.

"Well, that was only dogs and Billy Blythe," said Cissy, somewhat shamefacedly; "that doesn't count, and besides I like it. Doing good has got to be something you don't like—teaching little brats their duty to their godfathers and godmothers, or distributing tracts which only make people stamp and swear and carry on."

"Isn't there something somewhere about helping the fatherless and the widow?" faltered Hugh John. He hated "talking good," but somehow he felt that Cissy was doing herself less than justice.

"Well, I don't suppose that the fox-terrier's pa does much for him," she said gaily; "but come along and I'll 'interjuce' you to your ally Billy Blythe."

So they walked along towards the camp in silence. It was a still, Sunday-like evening, and the bell of Edam town steeple was tolling for the six o'clock stay of work, as it had done every night at the same hour for over five hundred years. The reek of the burgesses' supper-fires was going up in a hundred pillar-like "pews" of tall blue smoke. Homeward bound humble bees bumbled and blundered along, drunk and drowsy with the heady nectar they had taken on board—strayed revellers from the summer-day's Feast of Flowers. Delicate little blue butterflies rose flurriedly from the short grass, flirted with each other a while, and then mounted into a yet bluer sky in airy wheels and irresponsible balancings.

"This is my birthday!" suddenly burst out Hugh John.

Cissy stopped short and caught her breath.

"Oh no—it can't be;" she said, "I thought it was next week, and they aren't nearly ready."

Whereat Cissy Cartar began most incontinently and unexpectedly to cry. Hugh John had never seen her do this before, though he was familiar enough with Prissy's more easy tears.

"Now don't you, Ciss," he said; "I don't want anything—presents and things, I mean. Just let's be jolly."

"Hu-uh-uh!" sobbed Cissy; "and Janet Sheepshanks told me it was next week. I'm sure she did; and I set them so nicely to be ready in time—more than two months ago, and now they aren't ready after all."

"What aren't ready?" said Hugh John.

"The bantam chickens," sobbed Cissy; "and they are lovely as lovely. And peck—you should just see them peck."

"I'd just as soon have them next week, or the next after that—rather indeed. Shut up now, Ciss. Stop crying, I tell you. Do you hear?" He was instinctively adopting that gruff masculine sternness which men consider to be on the whole the most generally effective method of dealing with the incomprehensible tears of their women-kind. "I don't care if you cry pints, but I'll hit you if you won't stop! So there!"

Cissy stopped like magic, and assumed a distant and haughty expression with her nose in the air, the surprising dignity of which was marred only by the recurring spasmodic sniff necessary to keep back the moisture which was still inclined to leak from the corners of her eyes.

"I would indeed," said Hugh John, like all good men quickly remorseful after severity had achieved its end. "I'd ever so much rather have the nicest presents a week after; for on a regular birthday you get so many things. But by next week, when you've got tired of them all, and don't have anything new—that's the proper time to get a present."

"Oh, you are nice," said Cissy impulsively, coming over to Hugh John and clasping his arm with both her hands. He did not encourage this, for he did not know where it might end, and the open moor was not by any means the ivy-grown corner of the stable. Cissy went on.

"Yes, you are the nicest thing. Only don't tell any body——"

"I won't!" said Hugh John, with deepest conviction.

"And I'll give you the mother too," continued Cissy; "she is a perfect darling, and won a prize at the last Edam show. It was only a second, but everybody said that she ought by rights to have had the first. Yes, and she would have got it too—only that the other old hen was a cousin of the judge's. That wasn't fair, was it?"

"Certainly not!" said Hugh John, with instant emphasis.

CHAPTER XXVIII

THE GIPSY CAMP.

AT this point a peculiar fragrance was borne to them upon the light wind, the far-blowing smell of a wood-fire, together with the odour of boiling and fragrant stew—a compound and delicious wild-wood scent, which almost created the taste by which it was to be enjoyed, as they say all good literature must. There was also another smell, less idyllic but equally characteristic—the odour of drying paint. All these came from the camp of the gipsies set up on the corner of the common lands of Windy Standard.

The gipsies' wood was a barren acre of tall, ill-nurtured Scotch firs, with nothing to break their sturdy monotony of trunk right up to the spreading crown of twisted red branches and dark green spines. Beneath, the earth was covered with a carpet of dry and brown pine-needles, several inches thick, soft and silent under the feet as velvet pile. Ditches wet and dry closed in the place of sanctuary for the wandering tribes of Egypt on all sides, save only towards the high road, where a joggly, much-rutted cart track led deviously in between high banks, through which the protruding roots of the Scotch firs, knotted and scarred, were seen twisting and grappling each other like a nest of snakes. Suddenly, between the ridges of pine-trees, the pair came in sight of the camp.

"I declare," cried Hugh John, "they are painting the waggons. I wish they would let me help. I can slick it on like a daisy. Now I'm telling you. Andrew Penman at the coach-works in Church Street showed me how. He says I can 'line' as well as any workman in the place. I'm going to be a coach-painter. They get bully wages, I tell you."

"I thought you were going to be a soldier," commented Cissy, with the cool and inviting criticism of the model domestic lady, who is always on hand with a bucket of cold water for the enthusiasms of her men-folk.

Hugh John remembered, saw his mistake, and shifted his ground all in the twinkling of an eye; for of course a man of spirit ought never to own himself in the wrong—at least to a girl. It is a bad precedent, occasionally even fatal.

"Oh yes, of course I am going to be a soldier," he said with the hesitation of one who stops to think what he is going to say; "but I'm to be a coach-painter in my odd time and on holidays. Besides, officers get so little pay now-a-days, it's shameful—I heard my father say. So one must do something."

"Oh, here's the terrier—pretty thing, I declare he quite knows me—see, Hugh John," cried Cissy, kneeling with delight in her eye, and taking hold of the little dog, which came bounding forward to meet her—stopping midway, however, to paw at its neck, to which the Chianti wicker-work still clung tightly round the edge of the bandage.

Billy Blythe came towards them, touching his cap as he did so in a half-military manner; for had he not a brother in the county militia, who was the best fighter (with his fists) in the regiment, the pest of his colonel, but in private the particular pet of all the other officers, who were always ready to put their money on Gipsy Blythe to any amount.

"Yes, miss," he said; "I done it. He's better a'ready, and as lively as a green grass-chirper. Never seed the like o' that ointment. 'Tis worth its weight in gold when ye have dogs."

A tall girl came up at this moment, dusky and lithe, her face and neck tanned to a fine healthy brown almost as dark as saddle-leather, but with a rolling black eye so full and piercing that even her complexion seemed light by comparison. She carried a back load of tinware of all sorts, and by her wearied air appeared to be returning to the encampment after a day's tramp.

"Ah, young lady and gentleman, sure I can see by your eyes that you are going to buy something from a poor girl—ribbons for the hair, or for the house some nice collanders, saucepans, fish-pans, stew-pans, patty-pans, jelly-pans——"

"SHE CARRIED A BACK LOAD OF TINWARE."

"Go 'way, Lepronia Lovell," growled Billy; "don't you see that this is the young lady that cured my dog?"

"And who may the young gentleman be?" said the girl. "Certain I am I've seen him before somewhere at the back o' beyant."

"Belike aye, Lepronia, tha art a clever wench, and hast got eyes in the back o' thee yead," said Billy, in a tone of irony. "Do you not know the son of Master Smith o' t' Windy Standard—him as lets us bide on his land, when all the neighbours were on for nothing else but turning us off with never a rest for the soles of our feet?"

"And what is his name?" said the girl.

"Why, the same as his father of course, lass—what else?" cried Billy; "young Master Smith as ever was. Did you think it was Blythe?"

"'Faith then, God forbid!" said Lepronia, "ye have lashin's of that name in them parts already. Sure it is lonesome for a poor orphan like me among so many Blythes; and good-looking young chaps some o' them too, and never a wan o' ye man enough to ask me to change my name, and go to church and be thransmogrified into a Blythe like the rest of yez!"

Some of the gipsies standing round laughed at the boldness of the girl, and Billy reddened. "I'm not by way of takin' up with no Paddy," he said, and turned on his heel.

"Paddy is ut," cried the girl indignantly after him, "'faith now, and it wad be tellin' ye if ye could get a daycent single woman only half as good lookin' as me, to take as much notice av the likes o' ye as to kick ye out of her road!"

She turned away, calling over her shoulder to Cissy, "Can I tell your fortune, pretty lady?"

Quick as a flash, Cissy's answer came back.

"No, but I can tell yours!"

The girl stopped, surprised that a maid of the Gentiles should tell fortunes without glass balls, cards, or even looking at the lines of the hand.

"Tell it then," she said defiantly.

"You will live to marry Billy!" she said.

Then Lepronia Lovell laughed a short laugh, and said, "Never while there's a daycent scarecrow in the world will I set up a tent-stick along with the likes of Billy Blythe!"

But all the same she walked away very thoughtful, her basketful of tinware clattering at her back.

After the fox-terrier had been examined, commented upon, and duly dressed, Billy Blythe walked with them part of the way homeward, and Hugh John opened out to him his troubles. He told him of the feud against the town boys, and related all the manifold misdeeds of the Smoutchies. All the while Billy said nothing, but the twitching of his hands and a peculiarly covert look about his dusky face told that he was listening intently. Scarcely had Hugh John come to the end of his tale when, with the blood mounting darkly to his cheeks, Billy turned about to see if he were observed. There was no one near.

"We are the lads to help ye to turn out Nipper Donnan and all his crew," he said. "Him and his would soon make short work of us gipsies if they had the rights of castle and common. Why, Nipper's father is what they call a bailie of their burgh court, and he fined my father for leaving his horses out on the roadside, while he went for a doctor when my mother was took ill a year past last November."

Hugh John had found his ally.

"There's a round dozen and more of us lads," continued Billy, "that 'ud make small potatoes and mince meat of every one of them, if they was all Nipper Donnans—which they ain't, not by a long sight. I know them. A fig for them and their flag! We'll take their castle, and we'll take it too in a way they won't forget till their dying day."

The gipsy lad was so earnest that Hugh John, though as much as ever bent upon conquering the enemy, began to be a little alarmed.

"Of course it's part pretending," he said, "for my father could put them out if we were to tell on them. But then we won't tell, and we want just to drive them out ourselves, and thrash them for stealing our pet lamb as well!"

"Right!" said Billy, "don't be afraid; we won't do more than just give them a blazing good hiding. Tell 'ee what, they'll be main sore from top to toe before we get through with 'em!"

CHAPTER XXIX

TOADY LION'S LITTLE WAYS.

THUS it was finally arranged. The castle was to be attacked by the combined forces of Windy Standard and the gipsy camp the following Saturday afternoon, which would give them the enemy in their fullest numbers. Notice would be sent, so that they could not say afterwards that they had been taken by surprise. General Napoleon Smith was to write the letter himself, but to say nothing in it about his new allies. That, as Cissy put it, "would be as good as a sixpenny surprise-packet to them."

So full was Hugh John of his new plan and the hope, now almost the certainty, of success, that when he went home he could not help confiding in Prissy—who, like a model housewife, was seated mending her doll's stockings, while Janet Sheepshanks attended to those of the elder members of the household.

She listened with quick-coming breath and rising colour, till Hugh John thought that his own military enthusiasm had kindled hers.

"Isn't it prime?—we'll beat them till they can't speak," said Hugh John triumphantly. "They'll never come back to our castle again after we finish with them."

But Priscilla was silent, and deep dejection gnawed dully at her heart.

"Poor things," she said thoughtfully; "perhaps they never had fathers to teach them, nor godfathers and godmothers to see that they learned their Catechism."

"Precious lot mine ever did for me—only one old silver mug!" snorted Hugh John.

Just then Toady Lion came in.

"Oh, Hugh John," he panted, in tremulous haste to tell some fell tidings, "I so sorry—I'se broked one of the cannons, and it's your cannon what I'se broked."

"What were you doing with my cannon?" inquired his brother severely.

"I was juss playin' wif it so as to save my cannons, and a great bid stone fell from the wall and broked it all to bits. I beg'oo pardon, Hugh John!"

"All right!" said Hugh John cheerfully; "you can give me one of yours for it."

Toady Lion stood a while silent, with a puzzled expression on his face.

"That's not right, Hugh John," he said seriously; "I saided that I was sorry, and I begged 'oo pardon. Father says then 'oo must fordiv me!"

"Oh, I'll forgive you right enough," said Hugh John, "after I get the cannon. It's all the same to me which cannon I have."

"But your cannon is broked—all to little bits!" said Toady Lion, trying to impress the fact on his brother's memory.

"Well, another cannon," said Hugh John—"I ain't particular."

"But the other cannons is all mine," explained Toady Lion, who has strong ideas as to the rights of property.

"No matter—one of them is mine now!" said his brother, snatching one out of his arms.

Toady Lion began to cry with a whining whimper that carried far, and with which in his time he had achieved great things.

It reached the ear of Janet Sheepshanks, busy at her stocking-mending, as Toady Lion intended it should.

"I declare," she cried, "can you not give the poor little boy what he wants? A great fellow like you pestering and teasing a child like that. Think shame of yourself! What is the matter, Arthur George?"

"Hugh John tooked my cannon!" whimpered that young Machiavel.

"Haven't got your cannon, little sneak!" said Hugh John under his breath.

"Won't give me back my cannon!" wailed Toady Lion still louder, hearing Janet beginning to move, and knowing well that if he only kept it up she would come out, and, on principle, instantly take his part. Janet never inquired. She had a theory that the elder children were always teasing and oppressing the younger, and she acted upon it—acted promptly too.

"I wants—" began Toady Lion in his highest key.

"Oh, take the cannon, sneak!" said Hugh John fiercely, "chucking" his last remaining piece of artillery at Toady Lion, for Janet was almost in the doorway now.

Toady Lion burst into a howl.

"Oo-oo-ooooh!" he cried; "Hugh John hitted me on the head wif my cannon——"

"Oh, you bad boy, wait till I catch you, Hugh Picton Smith," cried Janet Sheepshanks, as the boy retreated precipitately through the open French window,—"you don't get any supper to-night, rascal that you are, never letting that poor innocent lamb alone for one minute."

In the safety of the garden walk Hugh John shook his fist at the window.

"Oh, golly," he said aloud; "just wait till Toady Lion grows up a bit. By hokey, won't I take this out of him with a wicket? Oh no—not at all!"

Now Toady Lion was not usually a selfish little boy; but this day it happened that he was cross and hot, also he had a tooth which was bothering him. And most of all he wanted his own way, and had a very good idea how to get it too.

That same night, when Hugh John was wandering disconsolately without at the hour of supper, wondering whether Janet Sheepshanks meant to keep her word, a small stout figure came waddling towards him. It was Toady Lion with the cover of a silver-plated fish-server in his hand. It was nearly full of a miscellaneous mess, such as children (and all hungry persons) love—half a fried sole was there, three large mealy potatoes, green peas, and a whole boiled turnip.

"Please, Hugh John," said Toady Lion, "I'se welly solly I broked your cannon. I bringed you mine supper. Will 'oo forgive me?"

"All right, old chap," said the generous hero of battles instantly, "that's all right! Let's have a jolly feed!"

So on the garden seat they sat down with the fish-cover propped between them, and ate their suppers fraternally and happily out of one dish, using the oldest implements invented for the purpose by the human race.

CHAPTER XXX

SAINT PRISSY, PEACEMAKER.

THIS is the letter which, according to his promise, General Napoleon Smith despatched to the accredited leader of the Smoutchy boys—or, as they delighted to call themselves, the Comanche Cowboys.

The reply came back on a piece of wrapping paper from the butcher's shop, rendered warlike by undeniable stains of gore. It had, to all appearance, been written with a skewer, and contrasted ill with the blue official paper purloined out of Mr. Picton Smith's office, on which the challenge had been sent. It ran thus:——

The high contracting parties having thus agreed upon terms of mutual animosity, to all appearance there remained only the arbitrament of battle.

But other thoughts were working in the tender heart of Prissy Smith. She had no sympathy with bloodshed, and had she been in her father's place she would at once have given the town all their desires at any price, in order that the peace might be kept. Deeply and sincerely she bewailed the spirit of quarrelling and bloodshed which was abroad. She had her own intentions as to the enemy, Hugh John had his—which he had so succinctly summed up in the "favour of the 13th," acknowledged with such businesslike precision by Mr. Nipper Donnan in his reply to General Napoleon's blue official cartel.

Without taking any one into her confidence (not even Sammy Carter, who might have laughed at her), Priscilla Smith resolved to set out on a mission of reconciliation to the Comanche Cowboys. Long and deeply she prepared herself by self-imposed penances for the work that was before her. She was, she knew, no Joan of Arc to lead an army in battle array against a cruel and taunting enemy. She was to be a St. Catherine of Siena rather, setting out alone and unfriended on a pilgrimage of mercy. She had read all she could lay her hands on about the tanner's daughter, and a picture of the great barn-like brick church of San Dominico where she had her visions, hung over the wash-stand in Prissy's little room, and to her pious eyes made the plain deal table seem the next thing to an altar.

Prissy wanted to go and have visions too; and so, three times a day she went in pilgrimage to the tool-house where the potatoes were stored, as being the next best thing to the unattainable San Dominico. This was a roomy place more than half underground, and had a vaulted roof which was supported by pillars—the remains, doubtless, of some much more ancient structure.

Here Prissy waited, like the Scholar Gipsy, for the light from heaven to fall; but, alas, the light refused to come to time. Well, then, she must just go on without it as many another eager soul had done before her. There only remained to make the final preparations.

On the morrow therefore she waited carefully after early dinner till General Smith and Toady Lion had gone off in the direction of the mill-dam. Then she took out the little basket which she had concealed in the crypt of San Dominico—that is to say in the potato house. It stood ready packed and covered with a white linen cloth.

It was a basket which had been prepared upon the strictest missionary models. She had no printed authorities which went the length of telling her what provision for the way, what bribes and presents Saint Catherine carried forth to appease withal the enemies of her city and country. But there was on record the exact provision of the mission-chest of a woman, who in her time went forth to turn to gentleness the angry hearts of brigands and robbers—one Abigail, the wife of a certain churl of Maon, a village near to the roots of Mount Carmel.

True, Prissy could not quite make up the tale of her presents on the same generous and wholesale scale. She had to preach according to her stipend, like the Glasgow wife of the legend, who, upon the doctor ordering her husband champagne and oysters, informed a friend that "poor folk like us couldna juist gie Tammas champeen-an'-ighsters, but we did the next best thing—we gied him whelks-an'-ginger-beer."

So since it might have attracted some attention, even on pastures so well stocked as those of Mr. Picton Smith of Windy Standard, if Prissy had taken with her "five sheep ready dressed," she had to be content with half of a sheep's-head-pie, which she had begged "to give away" from Janet Sheepshanks. To this she added a four pound loaf she had bought in Edam with her own money (Abigail's two hundred being distinctly out of her reach)—together with the regulation cluster of raisins and cake of figs which were both well within her means. In addition, since Prissy was a strict teetotaler, she took with her a little apparatus for making tea, some sugar and cream from the pantry, and her largest and best set of dolls' cups and saucers.

All this occupied a good deal of room and was exceedingly heavy, so that Prissy had very often to rest on the way towards the castle. She might have failed altogether, but that she saw Mike raking the gravel of the path near the edge of the water, and asked him to carry the basket for her over the stepping-stones.

Prince Michael, who as he often remarked was "spoiling for another taste of Donnybrook," conveyed the basket over Edam Water for his young mistress, without the least idea of the strange quest upon which the girl was going.

He laid it down and looked at the linen cover.

"Faix," he said, "sure 'tis a long road to sind a young lady wid a heavy load like that!"

Now, this was his mode of inviting an explanation, but Prissy was far too wise to offer one. She merely thanked him and went on her way towards the castle.

"Don't go near thim ruins till after Saturday, when we will clean every dirty spalpeen out of the place like thunder on the mountains," cried Mike, who, like some other people, loved to round off his sentences with sounding expressions without troubling himself much as to whether they fitted the place or not.

"Thank you!" cried Prissy over her shoulder, with a sweet and grateful, but quite uninforming smile.

She continued on her way till Mike was out of sight, without altering her course from the straight road to the wooden bridge which led into the town of Edam. Then at the edge of the hazel copse she came upon a small footpath which meandered through lush grass meadows and patches of the greater willow herb to the Castle of Windy Standard. The willow herb flourished in glorious red-purple masses on the ancient masonry of the outer defences, for it is a plant which loves above all things the disintegrating lime of old buildings from which its crown of blossom shoots up three or four, or it may be even six feet.

She skirted the moat, green with the leaves of pond-weed floating like small veined eggs on the surface. From the sluggish water at the side, iris and bog-bean stood nobly up, and white-lilies floated on the still surface in lordly pride among the humbler wrack and scum of duckweed and water buttercup. The light chrome heads of "Go-to-bed-John" flaunted on the dryer bank beyond.

Prissy eyed all these treasures with anxious glances.

"I want just dreadfully to gather you," she said. "I hope all this warring and battling will be over before you have done blooming, you nice waterside things."

And indeed I agree with her, for there is nothing much nicer in the world than wayside and riverside flowers—except the little children who play among them; and nothing sweeter than a bairns' daisy-chain, save the fingers which weave it, and the neck about which it hangs.

Prissy had arrived within sight of the castle now. She saw the flaunting of the red republican flag which in staggery capitals condemned her parent to instant dissolution. She stood a moment with the basket on her arm in front of the great ruined gate. A sentry was pacing to and fro there. Bob Hetherington was his name, and there were other lads and boys lounging and pretending to smoke in the deep embrasures and recesses of the walls. Clearly the castle was occupied in force by the enemy.

Prissy stopped somewhat embarrassed, and set down her basket that she might have a good look, and think what she was to do next. As she did so she caught the eye of Nosie Cuthbertson, a youth whom Nipper Donnan permitted in his corps because his father had a terrier which was undoubtedly the best ratter in Edam. But the privilege of association with such a distinguished dog was dear at the price, for no meaner nor more "ill-set" youth than Nosie Cuthbertson cumbered honest Bordershire soil. Nosie was seated trying to smoke dry dock-leaf wrapped in newspaper without being sick, when his eye caught the trim little figure on the opposite side of the moat.

"Hey, boys!" he cried, "here's the Smith lass. Let's go and hit her!"

Now Master Nosie had not been prominent on the great day of the battle of the Black Sheds, but he felt instinctively that against a solitary girl he had at last some chance to assert himself. So he threw away his paper cigar, and ran round the broken causeway to the place where Prissy was standing.

"'OH, PLEASE DON'T, SIR!'"

"If you please, sir," began Prissy sweetly, "I've come to ask you not to fight any more. It isn't right, you know, and God will be angry."

Nosie Cuthbertson did not at all attend to the appeal so gently and courteously made to him. He only caught Prissy by the hand, and began twisting her wrist and squeezing her slender fingers till the joints ground against each other, and Prissy bit her lips and was ready to cry with pain.

"Oh, please don't, sir!" she pleaded softly, trying to smile as at a famous jest. "I came because I wanted to speak to your captain, and I've brought a lot of nice things for you all. I think you will be sure to like them."

"Humbug," cried Nosie Cuthbertson, performing another yet more painful twist, "the basket's ours anyway. I captured it. Hey, Bob, catch hold of this chuck, while I give the girl toko—I'll teach her to come spying here about our castle!"

CHAPTER XXXI

PRISSY'S PICNIC.

BUT just at this moment an important personage stalked through the great broken-down doorway by which kings and princes most magnificent had once entered the ancient Castle of the Lorraines. He stood a moment or two on the threshold behind Nosie Cuthbertson, silently contemplating his courageous doings.

Presently a little stifled cry escaped from Prissy, caused by one of Nosie's refinements in torture, which consisted in separating her fingers and pulling two in one direction and two in the other. Nosie was a youth of parts and promise, who had already proceeded some distance on his way to the gallows.

But the Important Personage, who was no other than Nipper Donnan himself, did not long remain quiescent. He advanced suddenly, seized Nosie Cuthbertson by the scruff of the neck, kicked him several times severely, tweaked his ear till it looked as if it had been constructed of the best india-rubber, and then ended by tumbling him into the moat, where he disappeared as noiselessly as if he had fallen into green syrup.

"Now, what's all this?" cried the lordly Nipper, whose doings among his own no man dared to question, for reasons connected with health. At the first sight of him Bob Hetherington had quietly shouldered his musket, and begun pacing up and down with his nose in the air, as if he had never so much as dreamed of going near Prissy's basket.

"What's all this, I say—you?" demanded his captain.

"I don't know any bloomin' thing about it——" began Bob, with whom ignorance, if not honesty, was certainly the best policy.

"Salute!" roared his officer; "don't you know enough to salute when you speak to me? Want to get knocked endways?"

Sulkily Bob Hetherington obeyed.

"Well?" said Nipper Donnan, somewhat appeased by the appearance of Nosie Cuthbertson as he scrambled up the bank, with the green scum of duckweed clinging all over him. He was shaking his head and muttering anathemas, declaring what his father would do to Nipper Donnan, when within his heart he knew that first of all something very painful would be done to himself by that able-bodied relative as soon as ever he showed face at home.

"This girl she come to the drawbridge and hollered—that's all I know!" said the sentry, disassociating himself from any trouble as completely as possible. Bob felt that under the circumstances it was very distinctly folly to be wise. "I don't know what she hollered, but Nosie he runs an' begins twisting her arm, and then the girl she begins to holler again!"

"I didn't mean to," said Prissy tremulously, "but he was hurting so dreadfully."

"Come here, you!" shouted Nipper to the retiring Nosie. Whereupon that young gentleman, hearing the dreadful voice of his chief officer, and being at the time on the right side of the moat, did not pause to respond, but promptly took to his heels in the direction of the town.

"Run after him and bring him back, two of you fellows! Don't dare come back without him!"

cried Nipper, and at his word two big boys detached themselves from the doorposts in which the guard was kept, and dashed after the deserter.

"Oh, don't hurt him—perhaps he didn't mean it!" cried the universally sympathetic Prissy. "He didn't hurt me much after all, and it is quite better now anyway."

Nipper Donnan could, as we know, be as cruel as anybody, but he liked to keep both the theory and practice of terror in his own hands. Besides, some possible far-off fragrance from another life stirred in him when he saw the slim girlish figure of Prissy Smith, clad all in white with a large sun-bonnet edged with pale green, standing on the bank and appealing to him with eyes different from any he had ever seen. He wanted, he knew not why, to kick Nosie Cuthbertson— kick him much harder than he had done before he saw whom he was tormenting. He had never particularly noticed any one's eyes before. He had thought vaguely that every one had the same kind of eyes.

"THE RETURN OF THE TWO SWIFT FOOTMEN."

"Well, what do you want?" he said gruffly. For with Nipper and his class emotion or shamefacedness of any kind always in the first instance produces additional dourness.

Prissy smiled upon him—a glad, confident smile. She was the daughter of one war chief, the sister of another, and she knew that it is always best and simplest to treat only with principals.

"You know that I didn't come to spy or find out anything, don't you?" she said; "only I was so sorry to think you were fighting with each other, when the Bible tells us to love one another. Why can't we all be nice together? I'm sure Hugh John would if you would——"

"Gammon—this is our castle," said Nipper Donnan sullenly, "my father he says so. Everybody says so. Your father has no right to it."

"Well, but—" replied Prissy, with woman's gentle wit avoiding all discussion of the bone of contention, "I'm sure you would let us come here and have picnics and things. And you could come too, and play at soldiers and marching and drills—all without fighting to hurt."

"Fighting is the best fun!" snarled Nipper; "besides, 'twasn't us that begun it."

"Then," answered Prissy, "wouldn't it be all the nicer of you if you were to stop first?"

But this Nipper Donnan could not be expected to understand. A diversion was caused at this moment by the return of the two swift footmen, with the culprit Nosie between them, doing the frog's march, and having his own experiences as to what arm-twisting meant.

"Cast him into the deepest dungeon beneath the castle moat!" thundered the brigand chief.

"Can't," said the elder of the two captors, one Joe Craig, the son of the Carlisle carrier; "can't— we couldn't get him out again if we did!"

"Well then,"—returned the great chief, swiftly deciding upon an alternative plan, as if he had thought about it from the first, "chuck him down anywhere on the stones, and get Fat Sandy to sit on him."

"HYDRAULIC PRESSURE."

Joe Craig obediently saluted, and presently sundry moans and sounds of exhausted breath indicated that Nosie Cuthbertson was being subjected to hydraulic pressure by the unseen tormentor whom Nipper Donnan had called Fat Sandy. Prissy felt that nothing she could say would for the present lessen Master Nosie's griefs, so she went on to accomplish her purpose by other means.

"If you please, Mr. Captain," she said politely, "I thought you would like to taste our nice sheep's-head-pie. Janet makes it all out of her own head. Besides, there are some dee-licious fruits which I have brought you; and if you will let me come in, I will make you some lovely tea?"

Nipper Donnan considered, and at last shook his head.

"I don't know," he said, "'tisn't regular. How do we know that you aren't a spy?"

"You could bind my eyes with a napkin, and——"

"That's the thing!" cried several of Nipper's followers, who scented something to eat, and who knew that the commissariat was the weak point in the defences of the Castle of Windy Standard under the Consulship of Donnan.

"Well," said the chief, "that's according to rule. Here, Timothy Tracy, tell us if that is all right."

Whereupon uprose Timothy Tracy, a long lank boy with yellowish hair and dull lack-lustre eyes, out of a niche in the wall and unfolded a number of "The Wild Boys of New York." He rustled the flaccid, ill-conditioned leaves and found the place.

"'Then Bendigo Bill went to the gateway of the stockade to interview the emissary of the besiegers. With keen unerring eyes he examined his credentials, and finding them correct, he took from the breast of his fringed buckskin hunting-dress a handkerchief of fine Indian silk, and with it he swathed the eyes of the ambassador. Then taking the envoy by the hand he led him past the impregnable defences of the Comanche Cowboys into the presence of their haughty chief, who was seated with the fair Luluja beside him, holding her delicate hand, and inhaling the fragrance of a choice Havanna cigar through his noble aquiline nose.'

"That's all it says," said Timothy Tracy, succinctly, and straightway curled himself up again to resume his own story at the place where he had left it off.

"Well, that's all pretty straight and easy. Nobody can say fairer nor that," meditated Bob Hetherington.

"Shut up!" said his chief; "who asked for your oar? I'll knock the bloomin' nut off you if you don't watch out. Blindfold the emissary of the enemy, and bring her before me into the inner court."

And with this peremptory command, Nipper Donnan disappeared.

But the order was more easily given than obeyed. For not only could the entire array of the Comanche Cowboys produce nothing even distantly resembling Indian silk (which at any rate was a counsel of perfection), but what was worse, their pockets were equally destitute of common domestic linen. Indeed the proceedings would have fallen through at this point had not the ambassadress offered her own. This was knotted round her brows by Joe Craig, with the best intentions in the world.

Immediately after completing the arrangement, he stepped in front of Prissy and said, thrusting his fist below her nose, "Tell me if you see anything—mind, true as 'Hope-you-may-Die!'"

"I do see something, something very dirty," said Prissy, "but I can't quite tell what it is."

"She can see, boys," cried Joe indignantly, "it's my hand."

Every boy recognised the description, and the handkerchief was once more adjusted with greater care and precision than before, so that it was only by the sense of smell that Prissy could judge of the proximity of Joe Craig's fingers.

"Please let me carry my basket myself—I've got my best china tea-service in it—and then I will be sure that it won't get broken."

A licentious soldiery was about to object, but a stern command issued unexpectedly from one of the arrow-slits through which their chief had been on the watch.

"Give the girl the basket! Do you hear—you?"

And in this manner Prissy entered the castle, guarded on either side by soldiers with fixed (wooden) bayonets. And at the inner and outer ports, the convoy was halted and asked for the pass-word.

"Death!" cried Joe Craig, at the pitch of his voice.

"Vengeance!" replied the sentry. "Pass, 'Death'!"

At last Prissy felt the grass beneath her feet, and the handkerchief being slipped from her eyes, she found herself within the courtyard of the castle. The captain of the band sat before her with a red sash tied tightly about his waist. By his side swung a butcher's steel, almost as long and twice as dangerous as a sword.

Prissy began her mission at once, to allow Captain Donnan no time to order her out again, or to put her into a dungeon, as he had done with Hugh John.

"I think we had better have tea first," she said. "Have you got a match-box?"

She could not have taken a better line. Nipper Donnan stepped down from his high horse at once. He put his hand into his pocket. "I have only fusees," he said grandly, "but perhaps they will do. You see regular smokers never use anything else."

"Oh yes, they will do perfectly," returned Prissy sweetly, "it is just to light the spirit-lamp. See how nicely it fits in. Isn't it a beauty? I got that from father on my birthday. Wasn't it nice of him?"

Nipper Donnan grunted. He never found any marked difference between his birthday and any other day. Nevertheless he stood by and assisted at the making of the tea, a process which interested him greatly.

"I shall need some more fresh spring water for so many cups," said Prissy, "I only brought the full of the kettle with me."

The chief slightly waved a haughty hand, which instantly impelled Joe Craig forward as if moved by a spring. "Bring some fresh water from the well!" he commanded.

Joe Craig took the tin dipper, and was marching off. Prissy looked distressed.

"What is it?" said the robber chief. Now Prissy did not want to be rude, but she had her feelings.

"Oh, please, Mr. Captain," she said, "his hands—I think he has perhaps been working——"

Nipper Donnan had no fine scruples, but he respected them in such an unknown quantity as this dainty little lady with the green trimmed sun-bonnet and the widely-opened eyes.

"Tracy, fetch the water, you lazy jaundiced toad!" he commanded. The sallow student rose unwillingly, and moved off with his face still bent upon the thrilling pages of "The Wild Boys of New York," which he held folded small in his hand for convenience of perusal.

Presently the tea being made, the white cloth was laid on the grass, and the entire company of the Smoutchy Boys crowded about, always excepting the sentinels at the east and west doors, who being on duty could not immediately participate. The sheep's-head-pie, the bread, the butter, the fruits were all set out in order, and the whole presented such an appearance as the inside of the Castle of Windy Standard had never seen through all its generations.

Prissy conducted herself precisely as if she had been dispensing afternoon tea to callers in the drawing-room, as, since her last birthday, her father had occasionally permitted her to do.

"Do you take sugar?" she asked, delicately poising a piece in the dolls' sugar-tongs, and smiling her most politefully conventional smile at Nipper Donnan.

The brigand chief had never been asked such a question before, and had no answer of the usual kind at hand. But he replied for all that.

"Rather!" he cried in a burst, "if the grocer's not lookin'!"

"I mean in your tea! Do you take sugar in your tea?"

Prissy was still smiling.

Nipper appeared to acquiesce. Two knobs of sugar were dropped in. The whipped cream out of the wide-mouthed bottle was spooned delicately on the top, and with a yet more charming smile the cup was passed to him. He held it between his finger and thumb, as an inquiring naturalist holds a rare beetle. Then he put it down on a low fragment of wall and looked at it.

"One lump or two?" queried Prissy again, graciously transferring her attentions to Joe Craig.

"Eh, what?" ejaculated that warrior. Prissy repeated her question.

"As many as I can get!" cried the boy.

So one by one the brigands were served, and the subdued look which rests upon a Sunday-school picnic at the hour of refreshment settled down upon them. The Smoutchy boy is bad and bold, but he does not like you to see him in the act of eating. His instinct is to get behind a wall, or into the thick of a copse and do it there. A similar feeling sends the sparrow with a larger crumb than the others into the seclusion of his nest among the ivy.

Nevertheless the bread and jam, the raisins, and the sheep's-head-pie disappeared 'like snow off a dyke.' The wonder of the thimbleful cups, continually replenished, grew more and more surprising; and, winking slyly at each other the Smoutchies passed them in with a touch of their caps to be filled and refilled again and again. Prissy kept the kettle beside her, out of which she poured the water brought by Timothy Tracy as she wanted it. The golden colour of the tea degenerated, but so long as a few drops of milk remained to mask the fraud from their eyes, the Smoutchies drank the warm water with equal relish.

"Besides it's so much better for your nerves, you know!" said Prissy, putting her action upon a hygienic basis.

At first the boys had been inclined to snatch the viands from the table-cloth, and there was one footprint on the further edge. But the iron hand of Nipper Donnan knocked two or three intruders sprawling, and after that the eatables were distributed as patiently and exactly as at a Lord Mayor's banquet.

"Please will you let that boy get up?—I think he must have been sat upon quite long enough now," said Prissy, who could not bear to listen to the uneasy groaning of the oppressed prisoner.

The chief granted the boon. The sitter and his victim came in and were regaled amicably from one plate. "Pieces" and full cups of tea were despatched to the distant sentinels, and finally the whole company was in the midst of washing up, when Prissy, who had been kneeling on the grass wiping saucers one by one, suddenly rose to her feet with a little cry.

"Oh, it is so dreadful—I quite forgot!"

The Smoutchies stood open-mouthed, some holding dishes, some with belated pieces of pie, some only with their hands in their pockets, but all waiting eagerly for the revelation of the dreadful thing which their hostess had forgotten.

"Why, we forgot to say grace!" she cried—"well, anyway I am glad I remembered in time. We can say it now. Who is the youngest?"

The boys all looked guiltily at each other. Prissy picked out a small boy of stunted aspect, but whose face was old and wizened. He had just put a piece of tobacco into his mouth to take away the taste of the tea.

"You say it, little boy," she said pointedly, and shut her eyes for him to begin.

The boy gasped, glanced once at his chief, and made a bolt for the door, through which he had fled before the sentinels had time to stop him. At the clatter Prissy opened her eyes.

"What is the matter with that boy? Couldn't he say grace? Didn't he remember the beginning? Well, you say it then——"

Nipper Donnan shook his head. He had a fine natural contempt for all religious services in the abstract, but when one was brought before him as a ceremony, his sense of discipline told him that it must somehow be valuable.

"Better say it yourself," he suggested.

Whereat Prissy devoutly clasped her hands and shut her eyes.

There was a smart smack and something fell over. Prissy opened her eyes, and saw a boy sprawling on the grass.

"Right," said Nipper Donnan cheerfully, "go ahead—Joe Craig laughed. I'll teach him to laugh except when I tell him to."

So Prissy again proceeded with a grace of her own composition:

"God bless our table, Bless our food; And make us stable, Brave and good."

After all was over Prissy left the Castle of Windy Standard, without indeed obtaining any pledge from the chief of the army of occupation, but not without having done some good. And she went forth with dignity too. For not only did the robber chieftain provide her with an escort, but he ordered the ramparts to be manned, and a general salute to be fired in her honour.

Prissy waved her hand vigorously, and had already proceeded a little way towards the stepping-stones, when she stopped, laid down her basket, and ran back to the postern gate. She took her little tortoise-shell card-case out of her pocket.

"Oh, I was nearly forgetting—how dreadfully rude of me!" she said, and forthwith pulled out a card on which she had previously written very neatly:

Miss Priscilla Smith

At Home Every Day

She laid it on the stones, and tripped away. "I'm sorry I have not my brother's card to leave also," she said, looking up at the brigand chief, who had been watching her curiously from a window.

"Oh," said Nipper Donnan, "we shall be pleased to see him if he drops in on Saturday—or any other time."

Then he waited till the trim white figure was some distance from the gateway before he took his cap from his head and waved it in the air.

"Three proper cheers for the little lady!" he cried.

And the grim old walls of the Castle of Windy Standard never echoed to a heartier shout than that with which the Smoutchy boys sped Miss Priscilla Smith, the daughter of their arch enemy, upon her homeward way.

Prissy poised herself on tiptoe at the entrance of the copse, and blew them a dainty collective kiss from her fingers.

"Thank you so much," she cried, "you are very kind. Come and see me soon—and be sure you stop to tea."

And with that she tripped swiftly away homeward with an empty basket and a happy heart.

That night in her little room before she went to sleep she read over her favourite text, "Blessed are the peace-makers, for they shall be called the children of God."

"Oh dear," she said, "I should so like to be one some day."

CHAPTER XXXII

PLAN OF CAMPAIGN.

SATURDAY morning dawned calm and clear after heavy rain on the hills, with a Sabbath-like peace in the air. The smoke of Edam rose straight up into the firmament from a hundred chimneys, and the Lias Coal Mine contributed a yet taller pillar to the skies, which bushed out at the top till it resembled an umbrella with a thick handle. Hugh John had been very early astir, and one of his first visits had been to the gipsy camp, where he found Billy Blythe with several others all clad in their tumbling tights, practising their great Bounding Brothers' act.

"Hello," cried Hugh John jovially, "at it already?"

"The mornin's the best time for suppling the jints!" answered Billy sententiously; "ask Lepronia Lovell, there. She should know with all them tin pans going clitter-clatter on her back."

"I'll be thankin' ye, Billy Blythe, to kape a tight holt on the slack o' that whopper jaw of yours. It will be better for you at supper-time than jeerin' at a stranger girl, that is arnin' her bite o' bread daycent. And that's a deal more than ye can do, aye, or anny wan like ye!"

And with these brave words, Lepronia Lovell went jingling away.

The Bounding Brothers threw themselves into knots, spun themselves into parti-coloured tops, turned double and treble somersaults, built human pyramids, and generally behaved as if they had no bones in any permanent positions throughout their entire bodies. Hugh John stood by in wonder and admiration.

"Are you afraid?" cried Billy from where he stood, arching his shoulders and swaying a little, as one of the supporters of the pyramid. "No?—then take off your boots." Hugh John instantly stood in his stocking soles.

"Up with him!" And before he knew it, he was far aloft, with his feet on the shoulders of the highest pair, who supported him with their right and left hands respectively. From his elevated perch he could see the enemy's flag flaunting defiance from the topmost battlements of the castle.

As soon as he reached the ground he mentioned what he had seen to Billy Blythe.

"We'll have it low and mean enough this night as ever was, before the edge o' dark!" said Billy, with a grim nod of his head.

The rains of the night had swelled the ford so that the stepping-stones were almost impracticable—indeed, entirely so for the short brown legs of Sir Toady Lion. This circumstance added greatly to the strength of the enemy's position, and gave the Smoutchies a decided advantage.

"They can't be at the castle all the time," said Billy; "why not let my mates and me go in before they get there? Then we could easily keep every one of them out."

This suggestion much distressed General Smith, who endeavoured to explain the terms of his contract to the gipsy lad. He showed him that it would not be fair to attack the Smoutchies except on Saturday, because at any other time they could not have all their forces in the field.

Billy thought with some reason that this was simple folly. But in time he was convinced of the wisdom of not "making two blazes of the same wasps' byke," as he expressed it.

"Do for them once out and out, and be done with it!" was his final advice.

Hugh John could not keep from thinking how stale and unprofitable it would be when all the Smoutchies had been finally "done for," and when he did not waken to new problems of warfare every morning.

According to the final arrangements the main attack was to be developed from the broadest part of the castle island below the stepping-stones. There were two boats belonging to the house of Windy Standard, lying in a boat-house by the little pier on the way to Oaklands. For security these were attached by a couple of padlocks to a strong double staple, which had been driven right through the solid floor of the landing-stage.

The padlocks were new, and the whole appeared impregnable to the simple minds of the children, and even to Mike and Peter Greg. But Billy smiled as he looked at them.

"Why, opening them's as easy as falling off a stool when you're asleep. Gimme a hairpin."

But neither Prissy nor Cissy Carter had yet attained to the dignity of having their hair done up, so neither carried such a thing about with them. Business was thus at a standstill, when Hugh John called to Prissy, "Go and ask Jane Housemaid to give us one."

"A good thick 'un!" called Billy Blythe after her.

The swift-footed Dian of Windy Standard had only been away a minute or two before she came flying back like the wind.

"She-won't-give-us-any-unless-we-tell-her-what-it-is-for!" she panted, all in one long word.

"Rats!" said Hugh John contemptuously, "ask her where she was last Friday week at eleven o'clock at night!"

The Divine Huntress flitted away again on winged feet, and in a trice was back with three hairpins, still glossy from their recent task of supporting the well-oiled hair of Jane Housemaid.

With quick supple hand Billy twisted the wire this way and that, tried the padlock once, and then deftly bent the ductile metal again with a pair of small pincers. The wards clicked promptly back, and lo! the padlock was hanging by its curved tongue. The other was stiffer with rust, but was opened in the same way. The besiegers were thus in possession of two fine transports in which to convey their army to the scene of conflict.

It was the plan of the General that the men under Billy Blythe should fill the larger of the two boats, and drop secretly down the left channel till they were close under the walls of the castle. The enemy, being previously alarmed by the beating of drums and the musketry fire on the land side, would never expect to be taken in the rear, and probably would not have a single soldier stationed there.

Indeed, towards the Edam Water, the walls of the keep rose thirty or forty feet into the air without an aperture wide enough to thrust an arm through. So that the need of defence on that side was not very apparent to the most careful captain. But at the south-west corner, one of the flanking turrets had been overthrown, though there still remained several steps of a descent into the water. But so high was the river on this occasion, that it lapped against the masonry of the outer defences. To this point then, apparently impregnable, the formidable division under Billy Blythe was to make its way.

There was nothing very martial about the appearance of these sons of the tent and caravan. The Bounding Brothers wore their trick dresses, and as for the rest, they were simply and comprehensively arrayed in shirt and trousers. Not a weapon, not a sash, not a stick, sword, nor gun broke the harmonious simplicity of the gipsy army.

Yet it was evident that they knew something which gave them secret confidence, for all the time they were in a state of high glee, only partially suppressed by the authority of their leader, and by the necessity for care in manning the boat with so large a crew. There were fourteen who were to adventure forth under Billy's pennon.

To the former assailants of the Black Sheds there had been added a stout and willing soldier from the gardens of Windy Standard,—a boy named Gregory (or more popularly Gregory's Mixture), together with a forester lad, who was called Craw-bogle Tam from his former occupation of scaring the crows out of the corn. Sammy Carter had been cashiered some time ago by the Commander-in-chief, but nevertheless he appeared with three cousins all armed with dog-whips, which Sammy assured Hugh John were the deadliest of weapons at close quarters. Altogether it was a formidable array.

The boat for the attack on the land side was so full that there remained no room for Toady Lion. That young gentleman promptly sat down on the landing-stage, and sent up a howl which in a few moments would certainly have brought down Janet Sheepshanks and all the curbing powers from the house, had he not been committed to the care of Prissy, with public instructions to get him some toffy and a private order to take him into the town, and keep him there till the struggle was over.

Prissy went off with Sir Toady Lion, both in high glee.

"I'se going round by the white bwidge—so long, everybody! I'll be at the castle as soon as you!" he cried as he departed.

Hugh John sighed a sigh of relief when he saw them safely off the muster-ground. Cissy, however, was coming on board as soon as ever the boat was ready to start. She had been posted to watch the movements of the household of Windy Standard, and would report at the last moment.

"All right," she cried from her watch-tower among the whins, "Prissy and Toady Lion are round the corner, and Janet Sheepshanks has just gone into the high garden to get parsley."

"Up anchors," cried Hugh John solemnly, "the hour has come!"

Mike and Billy tossed the padlock chains into the bottom of the boats and pushed off. There were no anchors, but the mistake was permissible to a simple soldier like General Napoleon Smith.

CHAPTER XXXIII

TOADY LION'S SECOND LONE HAND.

EDAM Water ran swiftly, surging and pushing southward on its way to the sea. It was brown and drumly with a wrack of twigs and leaves, snatched from the low branches of the hazels and alders which fringed its banks. It fretted and elbowed, frothing like yeast about the landing-place from which the two boat-loads were to set out for the attack.

General Napoleon Smith, equipped with sword and sash, sat in the stern of the first, in order to steer, while Prince Michael O'Donowitch stood on the jetty and held the boat's head. The others sat still in their places till the General gave the word. The eager soldiery vented their feelings in a great shout. Cissy Carter took her place with a flying leap just as the rope was cast off, and the fateful voyage began.

At first there was little to be done save in the way of keeping the vessel's head straight, for the Edam Water, swirling and brown with the mountain rains, hurried her towards the island with almost too great speed. With a rush they passed the wide gap between the unsubmerged stones of the causeway, at which point the boldest held his breath. The beach of pebbles was immediately beyond. But they were not to be allowed to land without a struggle; for there, directly on their front, appeared the massed forces of the enemy, occupying the high bluff behind, and prepared to prevent the disembarkation by a desperate fusillade of stones and turf.

It was in this hour of peril that the soldierly qualities of the leader again came out most strongly.

He kept the boat's head straight for the shore, as if he had been going to beach her, till she was within a dozen yards; then with a quick stroke of his steering oar he turned her right for the willow copses which fringed the island on the eastern side. The water had risen, so that these were sunk to half their height in the quick-running flood, and their leaves sucked under with the force of the current. But behind there was a quiet backwater into which Hugh John ran his vessel head on till she slanted with a gentle heave up on the green turf.

"Overboard every man!" he cried, and showed the example himself by dashing into the water up to the knees, carrying the blue ensign of his cause. The enemy had not expected this rapid flank movement, and waited only till the invaders had formed in battle array to retreat upon the castle, fearful perhaps of being cut off from their stronghold.

General-Field-Marshal Smith addressed his army.

"Soldiers," he said, "we've got to fight, and it's dead earnest this time, mind you. We're going to lick the Smoutchies, so that they will stay licked a long time. Now, come on!"

This brief address was considered on all hands to be a model effort, and worthy of the imitation of all generals in the face of the enemy. The most vulnerable part of the castle from the landward side was undoubtedly the great doorway—an open arch of some six feet wide, which, however, had to be approached under a galling cross fire from the ports at either side and from the lintel above.

"It's no use wasting time," cried the General; "follow me to the door."

And with his sword in his hand he darted valiantly up the steep incline which led to the castle. Cissy Carter charged at his left shoulder also sword in hand, while Mike and Peter, with Gregory's Mixture and the Craw Bogle, were scarcely a step behind.

Stones and mortar hailed down upon the devoted band; sticks and clods of turf struck them on their shoulders and arms. But with their teeth clenched and their heads bent low, the storming party rushed undauntedly upon their foes.

The Smoutchies had built a breast-work of driftwood in front of the great entrance, but it was so flimsy that Mike and his companions kicked it away in a moment—yet not before General Smith, light as a young goat, had overleaped it and launched himself solitary on the foe. Then, with the way clear, it was cut and thrust from start to finish.

First among the assailants General Smith crossed swords with the great Nipper Donnan himself. But his reserves had not yet come up, and so he was beaten down by three cracks on the head received from different quarters at the same time. But like Witherington in the ballad, he still fought upon his knees; and while Prince Michael and Gregory's Mixture held the enemy at bay with their stout sticks, the stricken Hugh John kept well down among their legs, and used his sword from underneath with damaging effect.

"Give them the point—cold steel!" he cried.

"Cowld steel it is!" shouted Prince Michael, as he brought down his blackthorn upon the right ear of Nipper Donnan.

"Cauld steel—tak' you that!" cried Peter Greg the Scot as he let out with his left, and knocked Nosey Cuthbert over backwards into the hall of the castle.

Thus raged in front the heady fight; and thus with their faces to the foe and their weapons in their hands, we leave the vanguard of the army of Windy Standard, in order that for a little we may follow the fortunes of the other divisions.

Yes, divisions is the word, that is to say Billy Blythe's gipsy division and—Sir Toady Lion.

For once more Toady Lion was playing a lone hand.

So soon as Prissy and he had been left behind, we regret to be obliged to report that the behaviour of the distinguished knight left much to be desired.

"Don't be bad, Toady Lion," said his sister, gently taking him by the hand; "come and look at nice picture-books."

"Will be bad," growled Toady Lion, stamping his little foot in impotent wrath; "doan want t' look at pitchur-books—want to go and fight! And I will go too, so there!"

And in his fiery indignation he even kicked at his sister Prissy, and threw stones after the boat in which the expedition had sailed. The gipsy division, which was to wait till they heard the noise of battle roll up from the castle island before cutting loose, took pity on Sir Toady Lion, and but for the special nature of the service required of them, they would, I think, have taken him with them.

"That's a rare well-plucked little 'un!" cried Joe Baillie. "See how he shuts his fists, and cuts up rough!"

"A little man!" said the leader encouragingly; "walks into his sister's shins, don't he, the little codger!"

"Let me go wif you, please," pleaded Toady Lion; "I'll kill you unless!—Kill you every one!" And his voice was full of bloodshed.

"Last time 'twas me that d'livered Donald, when they all runned away or got took prisoner; and now they won't even take me wif them!"

Billy regretfully shook his head. It would not do to be cumbered with small boys in the desperate mission on which they were going. The hope was forlorn enough as it was.

"Wait till we come back, little 'un," he said kindly; "run away and play with your sister."

Toady Lion stamped on the ground more fiercely than ever.

"Shan't stop and play wif a girl. If you don't let me come, I shall kill you."

And with sentiments even more discreditable, he pursued their boat as long as he could reach it with volleys of stones, to the great delight of the gipsy boys, who stimulated him to yet more desperate exertions with cries of "Well fielded!" "Chuck her in hard!" "Hit him with a big one!" While some of those in the stern pretended to stand shaking in deadly fear, and implored Toady Lion to spare them because they were orphans.

"Shan't spare none—shall kill 'oo every one!" cried the angry Toady Lion, lugging at a bigger stone than all, which he could not lift above three inches from the ground.

"Will smass 'oo with this, Billy Blythe—bad Billy!" he exclaimed, as he wrestled with the boulder.

"Oh, spare me—think of my family, Toady Lion, my pore wife and childer," pleaded Billy hypocritically.

"'Oo should have finked of 'oo fambly sooner!" cried Toady Lion, staggering to the water's edge with the great stone.

But at this moment the noise of the crying of those warring for the mastery came faintly up from the castle island. The rope that had been passed through the ring on the landing-stage and held ready in the hand of Billy Blythe, was loosened, and the second part of the besieging expedition went down with the rushing spate which reddened Edam Water. And as they fell away Billy stood up and called for three cheers for "little Toady Lion, the best man of the lot."

But Toady Lion stood on the shore and fairly bellowed with impotent rage, and the sound of his crying, "I'll kill 'oo! I'll kill 'oo dead!" roused Janet Sheepshanks, who was taking advantage of her master's absence to carry out a complete house-cleaning. She left the blanket-washing to see what was the matter. But Toady Lion, angry as he was, had sense enough to know that if Janet got him, he would be superintended all the morning. So with real alacrity he slipped aside into the "scrubbery," and there lay hidden till Janet, anxious that her maids should not scamp their house-work, was compelled to hurry back to the laundry to see that the blankets were properly washed.

After this there was but one thing to do, and so the second division, under Sir Toady Lion, did it. He resolved to turn the enemy's flank, and attack him with reinforcements from an entirely unexpected quarter. So, leaving Prissy to her own devices, he took to his heels, and his fat legs carried him rapidly in the direction of the town of Edam. Difficulties there were of course, such as the barrier of the white lodge gate, where old Betty lay in wait for him.

But Toady Lion circumnavigated Betty by going to the lodge-door and shouting with all his might, "Betty, come quick, p'raps they's some soldiers comin' down the road—maybe Tom's comin', 'oo come and look."

"Sodjers—where?—what?" cried old Betty, waking up hastily from her doze, and fumbling in her pocket for the gate-key.

Toady Lion was at her elbow when she undid the latch. Toady Lion charged past her with a yell. Toady Lion it was who from the safe middle of the highway made the preposterous explanation, "Oh no, they isn't no soldiers. 'Tis only a silly old fish-man wif a tin trumpet."

"Come back, sir, or I'll tell your father! Come back at once!" cried old Betty.

But she might shake her head and nod with her nut-cracker chin till the black beads on her lace "kep" tinkled. All was in vain. Toady Lion was out of reach far down the dusty main road along which the Scots Greys had come the day that Hugh John became a soldier. Toady Lion was a born pioneer, and usually got what he wanted, first of all by dint of knowing exactly what he did want, and then "fighting it out on that line if it took all summer"—or even winter too.

The road to the town of Edam wound underneath trees great and tall, which hummed with bees and gnats that day as Toady Lion sped along, his bare feet "plapping" pleasantly in the white hot dust. He was furtively crying all the time—not from sorrow but with sheer indignation. He hated all his kind. He was going to desert to the Smoutchies. He would be a Comanche Cowboy if they would have him, since his brother and Cissy Carter had turned against him. Nobody loved him, and he was glad of it. Prissy—oh! yes, but Prissy did not count. She loved everybody and everything, even stitching and dollies, and putting on white thread gloves when you went into town. So he ran on, evading the hay waggons and red farm-carts without looking at them, till in a trice he had crossed Edam Bridge and entered the town—in the glaring streets and upon the hot pavement of which the sunshine was sleeping, and which on Saturday forenoon had more than its usual aspect of enjoying a perpetual siesta.

The leading chemist was standing at his door, wondering if the rustic who passed in such a hurry could actually be on the point of entering the shop of his hated rival. The linen-draper at the corner under the town clock was divided between keeping an eye on his apprentices to see that they did not spar with yard sticks, and mentally criticising the ludicrous and meretricious window-dressing of his next-door neighbour. None of them cared at all for the small dusty boy with the tear-furrowed countenance who kept on trotting so steadily through the town, turned confidently up the High Street, and finally dodged into the path which led past the Black Sheds to the wooden bridge which joined the castle island to the butcher's parks. As he crossed the grass Toady Lion heard a wrathful voice from somewhere calling loudly, "Nipper! Nipper-r-r-r! Oh, wait till I catch you!"

For it chanced that this day the leading butcher in Edam was without the services of both his younger assistants—his son Nipper and his message boy, Tommy Pratt. Mr. Donnan had a new cane in his hand, and he was making it whistle through the air in a most unpleasant and suggestive manner.

"Get away out of my field, little boy—where are you going? What are you doing there?"

The question was put at short range now, for all unwittingly Sir Toady Lion had almost run into butcher Donnan's arms.

"Please I finks I'se going to Mist'r Burnham's house," explained Toady Lion readily but somewhat unaccurately; "I'se keepin' off the grass—and I didn't know it was your grass anyway, please, sir."

At the same time Toady Lion saluted because he also was a soldier, and Mr. Donnan, who in his untempered youth had passed several years in the ranks of Her Majesty's line, mechanically returned the courtesy.

"Why, little shaver," he said not unkindly, "this isn't the way to Mr. Burnham's house. There it is over among the trees. But, hello, talk of the—ahem—why, here comes Mr. Burnham himself."

Toady Lion clapped his hands and ran as fast as he could in the direction of the clergyman. Mr. Burnham was very tall, very soldierly, very stiff, and his well-fitting black coat and corded silk waistcoat were the admiration of the ladies of the neighbourhood. He was never seen out of doors without the glossiest of tall hats, and it was whispered that he had his trousers made tight about the calves on purpose to look like a dean. It was also understood in well-informed circles that he was writing a book on the eastward position—after which there would be no such thing as the Low Church. Nevertheless an upright, good, and, above all, kindly heart beat under the immaculate silk M. B. waistcoat; also strong capable arms were attached to the armholes of the coat which fitted its owner without a wrinkle. Indeed, Mr. Burnham had a blue jacket of a dark shade in which he had once upon a time rowed a famous race. It hung now in a glass cabinet, and was to the clergyman what Sambo Soulis was to General-Field-Marshal Smith.

But as we know, the fear of man dwelt not in Sir Toady Lion, and certainly not fear of his clergyman. He trotted up to him and said, "I wants to go to the castle. You come."

Now hitherto Mr. Burnham had always seen Sir Toady Lion as he came, with shining face and liberally plastered hair, from under the tender mercies of Janet Sheepshanks—with her parting monition to behave (and perhaps something else) still ringing in his ear.

So that it is no wonder that he did not for the moment recognise in the tear-stained, dust-caked face of the barefooted imp who addressed him so unceremoniously, the features of the son of his most prominent parishioner. He gazed down in mildly bewildered surprise, whereupon Toady Lion took him familiarly by the hand and reiterated his request, with an aplomb which had all the finality of a royal invitation.

"Take me to the castle on the island. I 'ants to go there!"

"And who may you be, little boy?"

"Don't 'oo know? 'Oo knows me when 'oo comes to tea at our house!" cried Toady Lion reproachfully. "I'se Mist'r Smiff's little boy; and I 'ants to go to the castle."

"Why do you want to go to the castle island?" asked Mr. Burnham.

"To find my bruvver Hugh John," said Toady Lion instantly.

The butcher had come up and stood listening silently, after having, with a certain hereditary respect for the cloth, respectfully saluted Mr. Burnham.

"This little boy wants to go on the island to find his brother," said the clergyman; "I suppose I may pass through your field with him?"

"Certainly! The path is over at the other side of the field. But I don't know but what I'll come along with you. I've lost my son and my message-boy too. It is possible they may be at the castle. "There is some dust being kicked up among the boys. I can't get my rascals to attend to business at all this last week or two."

And Mr. Donnan again caused his cane to whistle through the air in a way that turned Toady Lion cold, and made him glad that he was "Mr. Smift's little boy," and neither the son nor yet the errand-boy of the butcher of Edam.

Presently the three came to the wooden bridge, and from it they could see the flag flying over the battlements of the castle, and a swarming press of black figures swaying this way and that across the bright green turf in front.

"Hurrah—yonder they'se fightin'. Come on, Mist'r Burnham, we'll be in time yet!" shouted Toady Lion. "They saided that I couldn't come; and I've comed!"

Suddenly a far-off burst of cheering came to them down the wind. Black dots swarmed on the perilous battlements of the castle. Other black dots were unceremoniously pitched off the lower ramparts into the ditch below. The red and white flag of jacobin rebellion was pulled under, and a clamorous crowd of disturbed jackdaws rose from the turrets and hung squalling and circling over the ancient and lofty walls.

The conflict had indeed joined in earnest. The embattled foes were in the death grips; and, fearful lest he should arrive too late, Toady Lion hurried forward his reinforcements, crying, "Come on both of you! Come on, quick!" Butcher Donnan broke into a run, while Mr. Burnham, forgetting all about his silk waistcoat, clapped his tall hat on the back of his head and started forward at his best speed, Toady Lion hanging manfully on to the long skirts of his coat, as the Highlanders had clung to the cavalry stirrups at Balaclava till they were borne into the very floodtide of battle.

There were now two trump-cards in the lone hand.

CHAPTER XXXIV

THE CROWNING MERCY.

WE must now take up the story of the third division of the great expedition, the plan and execution of which so fully reflects the military genius of our distinguished hero; for though this part was carried out by Billy Blythe, the credit of the design, as well as the discovery of the means of carrying it out, were wholly due to General Napoleon Smith.

When the second boat swept loose and the futile anger of Sir Toady Lion had ceased to excite the laughter of the crew, the gipsy lads settled down to watching the rush of the Edam Water as it swept them along. They had, to begin with, an easier task than the first boat expedition. No enemy opposed their landing. No dangerous concealed stepping-stones had to be negotiated on the route they were to follow. Leaving all to the action of the current, they swept through the entrance to the wider branch, and presently ranged up alongside the deserted water-front of the ancient defences. They let the castle drop a little behind, and then rowed up into the eddy made by the corner of the fallen tower, where, on the morning of his deliverance, Hugh John had disturbed the slumbering sheep by so unexpectedly emerging from the secret passage.

Billy stepped on shore to choose a great stone for an anchor, and presently pulled the whole expedition alongside the fallen masonry, so that they were able to disembark as upon a pier.

The Bounding Brothers immediately threw several somersaults just to let off steam, till Billy cuffed them into something like seriousness.

"Hark to 'em," whispered Charlie Lee; "ain't they pitching it into them slick, over there on the other side. It's surely about our time to go at it."

"Just you shut up and wait," hissed Billy Blythe under his breath. "That's all your job just now."

And here, in the safe shelter of the ruined tower, the fourteen listened to the roar of battle surging, now high, now low, in heady fluctuations, turbulent bursts, and yet more eloquent silences from the other side of the keep.

They could distinguish, clear above all, the voice of General Smith, encouraging on his men in the purest and most vigorous Saxon.

"Go at them, boys! They're giving in. Sammy Carter, you sneak, I'll smash you, if you don't charge! Go it, Mike! Wire in, boys! Hike them out like Billy-O!"

And the Bounding Brothers, in their itching desire to take part, rubbed themselves down as if they had been horses, and softly squared up to each other, selecting the tenderest spots and hitting lightly, but with most wondrous accuracy, upon breast or chin.

"Won't we punch them! Oh no!" whispered Charlie Lee.

But from the way that he said it, he hardly seemed to mean what he said.

Just then came a tremendous and long continued gust of cheering from the defenders of the castle, which meant that they had cleared their front of the assailants. The sound of General Smith's voice waxed gradually fainter, as if he were being carried away against his will by the tide of retreat. Still at intervals he could be heard, encouraging, reproving, exhorting, but without the same glad confident ring in his tones.

Flags of red and white were waved from the ramparts; pistols (charged with powder only) were fired from embrasures, and the Smoutchies rent their throats in arrogant jubilation. They thought that the great assault had failed.

But behind them in the turret, all unbeknown, the Bounding Brothers silently patted one another with their knuckles as if desirous of practising affectionate greetings for the Smoutchies.

Perhaps they were; and then, again, perhaps they weren't.

"Now's our time," cried Billy Blythe; "come on, boys. Now for it!"

And with both hands and feet he began to remove certain flag-stones and recently heaped up débris from the mouth of a narrow passage, the same by which Hugh John had made his escape. His men stood around in astonishment and slowly dawning admiration, as they realised that their attack was to be a surprise, the most complete and famous in history, and also one strictly devised and carried out on the best models. Though the rank and file did not know quite so much about that as their Commander-in-Chief, who was sure in his heart that Froissart would have been glad to write about his crowning mercy.

It is one of the proofs of the genuine nobility of Hugh John's nature, and also of his consummate generalship, that he put the carrying out of the final coup of his great scheme into other hands, consenting himself to take the hard knocks, to be mauled and defeated, in order that the rout of the enemy might be the more complete.

The rubbish being at last sufficiently cleared, Billy bent his head and dipped down the steps. Charlie Lee followed, and the fourteen were on their way. Silently and cautiously, as if he had been relieving a hen-roost of its superfluous inhabitants, Billy crept along, testing the foothold at every step. He came to the stairway up to the dungeon, pausing a moment, to listen. There was a great pow-wow overhead. The Smoutchies were in the seventh heaven of jubilation over the repulse of the enemy.

Suddenly somebody in the passage sneezed.

Billy turned to Charlie Lee. "If that man does that again, burke him!" he whispered.

Then with a firm step he mounted the final ascent of the secret stair. His head hit hard against the roof at the top. He had not remembered how Hugh John had told him that the exit was under the lowest part of the bottle dungeon.

"Bless that roof!" he muttered piously—more piously, perhaps, than could have been expected of him, considering his upbringing.

"If Billy Blythe says that again, burke him!" said a carefully disguised gruff voice from the back—evidently that of the late sneezer.

"Silence—or by the Lord I'll slay you!" returned Billy, in a hissing whisper.

There was the silence of the grave behind. Billy Blythe made himself much respected for the moral rectitude and true worth of his character.

One by one the fourteen stepped clear of the damp stairs, and stood in the wide circuit of the dungeon.

But the narrow circular exit of the cell was still twelve feet above them. How were they to reach it? The walls were smooth as the inside of the bottle from which the prison-house took its name, curving in at the top, without foothold or niches in their smooth surface, so that no climber could ascend more than a few feet.

The Bounding Brothers stepped to the front, and with a hitch of their shoulders, stood waiting. "Ready!" said Billy.

In a moment Charlie Lee was balancing himself on the third storey of the fraternal pyramid. He could just look over the edge of the platform on which the mouth of the dungeon was placed. He ducked down sharply.

"THE LIVING CHAIN."

"They are all at their windows, yelling like fun," he whispered, with the white, eager look of battle on his face.

"Up, and at 'em!" said Billy, as if he had been the Great Duke.

And at his word the Bounding Brothers arched their shoulders to receive the weight of the coming climbers. One after another the remaining eleven scrambled up, swift and silent as cats; and with Charlie Lee at their head, lay prone on the dungeon platform, waiting the word of command. Close as herrings in a barrel they crouched, their arms outstretched before them, and their chins sunk low on the masonry.

Billy crept along till his head lay over the edge of the bottle dungeon. He extended his arms down. The highest Bounding Brother grasped them. His mate at the foot cast loose from the floor and swarmed up as on a ladder. The living chain swayed and dangled; but though his wrists ached as if they would part from their sockets, Billy never flinched; and finally, with Charlie Lee stretched across the hollow of his knees to keep all taut behind, by mere leverage of muscle he drew up the last brother upon the dungeon platform.

The fourteen lay looking over upon the unconscious enemy. The level of the floor of the keep was six feet below. The Smoutchies to a man were at their posts.

With a nudge of his elbow Billy intimated that it was not yet time for the final assault. He listened with one ear turned towards the great open gateway, till he heard again the rallying shout of General Napoleon Smith.

"Now then! Ready all! Double-quick! Char-r-r-ge!"

With a shout the first land division, once repulsed, came the second time at the foe. The Smoutchies crowded to the gateway, deserting their windows in order to repel the determined assault delivered by Hugh John and his merry men.

"Now!" said Billy Blythe softly, standing up on the dungeon platform.

He glanced about him. Every Bounding Brother and baresark man of the gipsy camp had the same smile on his face, the boxer's smile when he gives or takes punishment.

Down leaped Billy Blythe, and straight over the floor of the keep for the great gateway he dashed. One, two—one, two! went his fists. The thirteen followed him, and such was the energy of their charge that the Smoutchies, taken completely by surprise, tumbled off their platforms by companies, fell over the broken steps by platoons, and even threw themselves in their panic into the arms of Hugh John and his corps, who were coming on at the double in front.

Never was there such a rout known in history. The isolated Smoutchies who had been left in the castle dropped from window and tower at the peril of their necks in order that they might have a chance of reaching the ground in safety. Then they gathered themselves up and fled helter-skelter for the bridge which led towards the town of Edam.

But what completed their demoralisation was that at this psychological moment the third division under Sir Toady Lion came into action. Mr. Burnham, with his coat-tails flying, caught first one and then another, and whelmed them on the turf, while the valiant butcher of Edam, having secured his own offspring firmly by the collar, caused his cane to descend upon that hero's back and limbs till the air was filled with the resultant music. And the more loudly Nipper howled, the faster and faster the Smoutchies fled, while the shillelahs of the two generals, and the fists of the Bounding Brothers, wrought havoc in their rear. The flight became a rout. The bridge was covered with the fugitives.

The forces of Windy Standard took all the prisoners they wanted, and butcher Donnan took his son, who for many days had reason to remember the circumstance. He was a changed Smoutchy from that day.

The camp of the enemy, with all his artillery, arms, and military stores, fell into the hands of the triumphant besiegers.

At the intercession of Mr. Burnham the prisoners were conditionally released, under parole never to fight again in the same war—nor for the future to meddle with the Castle of Windy Standard, the property, as Hugh John insisted on putting it, of Mr. Picton Smith, Esq., J. P.

But Mr. Burnham did what was perhaps more efficacious than any oaths. He went round to all the parents, guardians, teachers, and employers of the Smoutchy army. He represented the state of the case to them, and the danger of getting into trouble with a man so determined and powerful as Mr. Picton Smith.

The fists of the Bounding Brothers, the sword of General Napoleon, the teeth and nails of Sir Toady Lion (who systematically harassed the rear of the fleeing enemy) were as nothing to the several interviews which awaited the unfortunate Smoutchies at their homes and places of business or learning that evening, and on the succeeding Monday morning. Their torture of General Smith was amply avenged.

The victorious army remained in possession of the field, damaged but happy. Their triumph had not been achieved without wounds and bruises manifold. So Mr. Burnham sent for half-a-crown's worth of sticking-plaster, and another half-crown's worth of ripe gooseberries.

Whereupon the three divisions with one voice cheered Mr. Burnham, and Toady Lion put his hand on the sacred silk waistcoat, and said in his most peculiar Toady-leonine grammar, "'Oo is a bwick. Us likes 'oo!"

Which Mr. Burnham felt was, at the very least, equivalent to the thanks of Parliament for distinguished service.

It was a very happy, a very hungry, a very sticky, and a very patchy army which approached the house of Windy Standard at six o'clock that night, and was promptly sent supperless to bed. Hugh John parted with Cissy at the stepping-stones. Her eyes dwelt proudly and happily upon him.

"You fought splendidly," she said.

"We all fought splendidly," replied Hugh John, with a nod of approval which went straight to Cissy's heart, so that the tears sprang into her eyes.

"Oh, you are a nice thing, Hugh John!" she cried impulsively, reaching out her hands to clasp his arm.

"No, I'm not!" said Hugh John, startled and apprehensive. Then without waiting for more he turned hastily away.

But all the same Cissy Carter was very happy that night as she went homeward, and did not speak or even listen when Sammy addressed her several times by the way upon the dangers of war and the folly of love.

CHAPTER XXXV

PRISSY'S COMPROMISE.

AFTER the turmoil and excitement of the notably adventurous days which ended with the capture of the castle, the succeeding weeks dragged strangely. The holidays were dwindling as quickly as the last grains of sand in an hourglass, and there was an uneasy feeling in the air that the end of old and the beginning of new things were alike at hand.

Mr. Picton Smith returned from London the day after the great battle. That afternoon he was closeted for a long time with Mr. Burnham, but not even the venturesome Sir Toady Lion on his hands and knees, could overhear what the two gentlemen had to say to each other. At all events Mr. Smith did not this time attempt to force any confession from the active combatants. His failure on a former occasion had been complete enough, and he had no desire once more to confess himself worsted by Hugh John's determination to abjure all that savoured even remotely of the "dasht-mean."

But it is certain that the Smoutchy ringleaders were not further punished, and Mr. Smith took no steps to enforce the interdict which he had obtained against trespassers on the castle island.

For it was about this time that Prissy, having taken a great deal of trouble to understand all the bearings of the case, at last, with a brave heart, went and knocked at her father's study door.

"Come in," said the deep grave voice instantly, sending a thrill through the closed door, which made her tremble and rather wish that she had not come.

"Saint Catherine of Siena would not have been afraid," she murmured to herself, and forthwith opened the door.

"Well, little girl, what is it? What can I do for you?" said her father, smiling upon her; for he had heard of her ambassadorial picnic to the Smoutchies, and perhaps his daughter's trustful gentleness had made him a little ashamed of his own severity.

Prissy stood nerving herself to speak the words which were in her heart. She had seen Peace and kindly Concord bless her mission from afar; and now, like Paul before King Agrippa, she would not be unfaithful to the heavenly vision.

"Father," she said at last, "you don't really want to keep people out of the castle altogether, do you?"

"Certainly not, if they behave themselves," said her father, "but the mischief is that they don't."

"But suppose, father, that there was some one always there to see that they did behave, would you mind?"

"Of course not," replied her father, "but you know, Prissy, I can't afford to keep a man down on the island to see that sixpenny trippers don't pull down my castle stone by stone, or break their own necks by falling into the dungeon."

Prissy thought a little while, and then tried a new tack.

"Father"—she went a little nearer to him and stroked the cuff of his coat-sleeve—"does the land beyond the bridge belong to you?"

Mr. Picton Smith moved away his hand. Her mother used to do just that, and somehow the memory hurt. Nevertheless, all unconsciously, the touch of the child's hand softened him.

"No, Prissy," he said wonderingly, "but what do you know about such things?"

"Nothing at all," she answered, "but I am trying to learn. I want everybody to love you, and think you as nice as I know you to be. Don't you think you could let some one you knew very well live in the little lodge by the white bridge, and keep out the horrid people, or see that they behaved themselves?"

"The town would never agree to that," said her father, not seeing where he was being led.

"Don't you think the town's people would if you gave them the sixpences all for themselves?"

Her father pushed back his chair in great astonishment and looked at Prissy.

"Little girl," he said very gravely, "who has been putting all this into your head? Has anybody told you to come to me about this?"

Prissy shook her head quickly, then she looked down as if embarrassed.

"Well, what is it? Go on!" said her father, but the words were more softly spoken than you would think only to see them printed.

"Nobody told me about anything—I just thought about it all myself, father," she answered, taking courage from a certain look in Mr. Smith's eyes; "once I heard you say that the money was what the town's-people cared about. And—and—well, I knew that Jane Housemaid wanted to get married to Tom Cannon, and you see they can't, because Tom has not enough wages to take a house."

Prissy was speaking very fast now, rattling out the words so as to be finished before her father could interpose with any grown-up questions or objections.

"And you know I remembered last night when I was lying awake that Catherine would have done this——"

"What Catherine?" said her father, who did not always follow his daughter's reasoning.

"Saint Catherine of Siena, of course," said Prissy, for whom there was no other of the name; "so I came to you, and I want you to let Tom and Jane have the cottage, and Jane can take up the sixpences in a little brass plate like the one Mr. Burnham gets from the churchwardens on Sunday. And, oh! but I would just love to help her. May I sometimes, father?"

"Well," said her father, laughing, "there is perhaps something in what you say; but I don't think the Provost and Magistrates would ever agree. Now run away and play, and I will see what can be done."

But all the same Prissy did not go and play, and it was not Mr. Picton Smith who saw what could be done. On the afternoon of the same day the Provost of the good town of Edam entered the Council Chamber wiping his face and panting vigorously. He was a stout man of much good humour when not crossed in temper, the leading chemist and druggist in the town, and as the proprietor of more houses and less education than any man in Edam, of very great influence among the councillors.

"Well, billies," he cried jovially, "what do you think? There's a lass has keep'd me from the meetin' of this council for a full half-hour."

"A lass!" answered the senior bailie, still more hilariously, "that's surely less than proper. I will be compelled to inform Mrs. Lamont of the fact."

"Oh, it was a lassie of twelve or thirteen," answered the Provost. "So none of your insinuations, Bailie Tawse, and I'll thank you. She had a most astonishing tale to tell. It appears she is Picton Smith's lassie from Windy Standard; and she says to me, says she, 'Provost, do you want to have the tourist folk that come to Edam admitted to the castle?' says she. 'Of course,' says I, 'that is what the law-plea is about. That dust is no settled yet.' 'Then,' says she, brisk as if she was hiring me at Yedam fair, 'suppose my father was willing to let ye charge a sixpence for admission, would you pay a capable man his wages summer and winter to look after it—a man that my father would approve of?' 'Aye,' says I, 'the council would be blythe and proud to do that'—me thinking of my sister's son Peter that was injured by a lamp-post falling against him last New Year's night as he was coming hame frae the Blue Bell. 'Then,' says she, 'I think it can be managed. My father will put Tom Cannon in the lodge at the white bridge. You will pay him ten shillings in the week for his wife looking after the gate and taking the parties over the castle.' 'His wife,' says I; 'Tom is no married that ever I heard.' 'No,' says she, 'but he will be very quick if he gets the lodge.' Then I thocht that somebody had put her up to all this, and I questioned her tightly. But no—certes, she is a clever lass. I verily believe if I had said the word she would hae comed along here to the council meeting and faced the pack o' ye. But I said to her that she might gang her ways hame, and that I would put the matter before the council mysel'!"

"'THEN,' SAID PRISSY, 'I THINK IT CAN BE MANAGED.'"

The Provost, who had been walking up and down all the time and wiping his brow, finally plumped solidly into his chair. There was a mighty discussion—in which, as usual, many epithets were bandied about; but finally it was unanimously agreed that, if the offer were put on a firm and legal basis and the interdict withdrawn, the "Smith's Lassie" compromise, as it was called for brevity, might be none such a bad solution of the difficulty for all parties.

Thus by the wise thought and brave heart of a girl was the great controversy ended. And now the tourist and holiday-maker, each after his kind, passes his sixpence into the slot of a clicking gate, instead of depositing it in the brazen offertory salver, which had been the desire of Prissy's heart.

"For," said one of the councillors generously, when the plate was proposed, "how do we know that Mrs. Cannon might not keep every second sixpence for herself—or maybe send it up to Mr. Smith? We all know that she was long a servant in his house. No, no, honesty is honesty—but it's better when well looked after. Let us have a patent 'clicker.' I have used one attached to my till for years, and found it of great utility in the bacon-and-ham trade."

But the change made no difference to Hugh John and no difference to Toady Lion; for they came and went to the castle by the stepping-stones, and Cissy Carter took that way too, leaping as nimbly as any of them from stone to stone.

On the Sunday after this was finally arranged, Mr. Burnham gave out his text:—

"Blessed are the peacemakers, for they shall be called the children of God."

And this is the way he ended his sermon: "There is one here to-day whom I might without offence or flattery call a true child of God. I will not say who that is; but this I will say, that I, for one, would rather be such a peacemaker, and have a right to be called by that other name, than be general of the greatest army in the world."

"I think he must mean the Provost—or else my father," said Prissy to herself, looking reverently up to where, in the front row of the upper seats, the local chief magistrate sat, mopping his head with a red spotted handkerchief, and sunning himself in the somewhat sultry beams of his own greatness.

As for Hugh John, he declared that for a man who could row in a college boat, and who worshipped an old blue coat hung up in a glass case, Mr. Burnham said more drivelling things than any man alive or dead.

And Toady Lion said nothing. He was only wondering all through the service whether he could catch a fly without his father seeing him.—He found that he could not. After this failure he remembered that he had a brandy ball only half sucked in his left trousers' pocket. He got it out with some difficulty. It had stuck fast to the seams, and finally came away somewhat mixed up with twine, sealing wax, and a little bit of pitch wrapped in leather. But as soon as he got down to it the brandy ball proved itself thoroughly satisfactory, and the various flavours developed in the process of sucking kept Toady Lion awake till the blessed "Amen" released the black-coated throng.

Toady Lion's gratitude was almost an entire thanksgiving service of itself.

As he came out through the crowded porch, he put his hand into his father's, and with a portentous yawn piped out in his shrillest voice, "Oh, I is so tired."

The smile which ran round the late worshippers showed that Toady Lion had voiced the sentiments of many of Mr. Burnham's congregation.

At this moment Mr. Burnham himself came out of the vestry just in time to hear the boy's frank expression of opinion.

"Never mind, Toady Lion," he said genially, "the truth is, I was a little tired myself to-day. I promise not to keep you quite so long next Sunday morning. You must remind me if I transgress. Nobody will, if you don't, Toady Lion."

"Doan know what 'twansguess' is—but shall call out loud if you goes on too long—telling out sermons and textises and fings."

As they walked along the High Street of Edam, Prissy glanced reverently at the Provost.

"Oh, I wish I could have been a peacemaker too, like him," she sighed, "and then Mr. Burnham might have preached about me. Perhaps I will when I grow up."

For next to Saint Catherine of Siena, the Provost was her ideal of a peacemaker.

As they walked homeward, Mr. Burnham came and touched Prissy on the shoulder.

"Money cannot buy love," he said, somewhat sententiously, "but you, my dear, win it by loving actions."

He turned to Toady Lion, who was trotting along somewhat sulkily, holding his sister's hand, and grumbling because he was not allowed to chase butterflies on Sunday.

"Arthur George," said Mr. Burnham, "if anybody was to give you a piece of money and say, 'Will you love me for half-a-crown,' you couldn't do it, could you?"

"Could just, though!" contradicted Toady Lion flatly, kicking at the stones on the highway.

"Oh no," his instructor suavely explained, "if it were a bad person who asked you to love him, you wouldn't love him for half-a-crown, surely!"

Toady Lion turned the matter over.

"Well," he said, speaking slowly as if he were thinking hard between the words, "it might have to be five sillin's if he was very bad!"

CHAPTER XXXVI

HUGH JOHN'S WAY-GOING.

THE secret which had oppressed society after the return of Mr. Picton Smith from London, being revealed, was that Hugh John and Sammy Carter were both to go to school. For a while it appeared as if the foundations of the world had been undercut—the famous fellowship of noble knights disbanded, Prissy and Cissy, ministering angel and wild tomboy, alike abandoned to the tender mercies of mere governesses.

Strangest of all to Prissy was the indubitable fact that Hugh John wanted to go. At the very first mention of school he promptly forgot all about his noblest military ambitions, and began oiling his cricket bat and kicking his football all over the green. Mr. Burnham was anxious about his pupil's Latin and more than doubtful about his Vulgar Fractions; but the General himself was chiefly bent on improving his round arm bowling, and getting that break from the left down to a fine point.

Every member of the household was more or less disturbed by the coming exodus—except Sir Toady Lion. On the last fateful morning that self-contained youth maundered about as usual among his pets, carrying to and fro saucers of milk, dandelion leaves cut small, and other dainties—though Hugh John's boxes were standing corded and labelled in the hall, though Prissy was crying herself sick on her bed, and though there was even a dry hard lump high up in the great hero's own manly throat.

His father was giving his parting instructions to his eldest son.

"Work hard, my boy," he said. "Tell the truth, never tell tales, nor yet listen to them. Mind your own business. Don't fight, if you can help it; but if you have to, be sure you get home with your left before the other fellow. Practise your bowling, the batting will practise itself. And when you play golf, keep your eye on the ball."

"I'll try to play up, father," said Hugh John, "and anyway I won't be 'dasht-mean'!"

His father was satisfied.

Then it was Prissy who came to say good-bye. She had made all sorts of good resolutions, but in less than half a minute she was bawling undisguisedly on the hero's neck. And as for the hero—well, we will not say what he was doing, something most particularly unheroic at any rate.

Janet Sheepshanks hovered in the background, saying all the time, "For shame, Miss Priscilla, think shame o' yoursel'—garring the laddie greet like that when he's gaun awa'!"

But even Janet herself was observed to blow her own nose very often, and to offer Hugh John the small garden hoe instead of the neatly wrapped new silk umbrella she had bought for him out of her own money.

And all the while Sir Toady Lion kept on carrying milk and fresh lettuce leaves to his stupid lop-eared rabbits. Yet it was by no means insensibility which kept him thus busied. He was only playing his usual lone hand.

Yet even Toady Lion was not without his own proper sense of the importance of the occasion.

"There's a funny fing 'at you wants to see at the stile behind the stable," he remarked casually to Hugh John, as he went past the front door with an armful of hay for bedding, "but I promised not to tell w'at it is."

Immediately Hugh John slunk out, ran off in an entirely different direction, circled about the "office houses," reached the stile behind the stable—and there, with her eyes very big, and her underlip quivering strangely, he discovered Cissy Carter.

He stopped short and looked at her. The pressure of having to say farewell, or of making a stated speech of any kind, weighed heavily upon him. The two looked at each other like young wild animals—or as if they were children who had never been introduced, which is the same thing.

"Hugh John Picton, you don't care!" sobbed Cissy at last. "And I don't care either!" she added haughtily, commanding herself after a pathetic little pause.

"I do, I do," answered Hugh John vehemently, "only every fellow has to. Sammy is going too, you know!"

"Oh, I don't care a button for Sammy!" was Cissy's most unsisterly speech.

Hugh John tried to think of something to say. Cissy was now sobbing quietly and persistently, and that did not seem to help him.

"Say, don't now, Ciss! Stop it, or you'll make me cry too!"

"You don't care! You don't love me a bit! You know you don't!"

"I do—I do," protested the hero, in despair, "there—there—now you can't say I don't care."

"But you'll be so different when you come back, and you'll have lost your half of the crooked sixpence."

"I won't, for true, Cissy—and I shan't ever look at another girl nor play horses with them even if they ask me ever so."

"You will, I know you will!"

A rumble of wheels, a shout from the front door—"Hugh John—wherever can that boy have got to?"

"Good-bye, Ciss, I must go. Oh hang it, don't go making a fellow cry. Well, I will say it then, 'I love you, Ciss!' There—will that satisfy you?"

"A SLIM BUNDLE OF LIMP WOE."

Something lit on the end of Cissy's nose, which was very red and wet with the tears that had run down it. There was a clatter of feet, and the Lord of Creation had departed. Cissy sank down behind the stone wall, a slim bundle of limp woe, done up in blue serge trimmed with scarlet.

The servants were gathered in the hall. Several of the maids were already wet-eyed, for Hugh John had "the way with him" that made all women want to "mother" him. Besides, he had no mother of his own.

"Good-bye, Master Hugh!" they said, and sniffed as they said it.

"Good-bye, everybody," cried the hero, "soon be back again, you know." He said this very loudly to show that he did not care. He was going down the steps with Prissy's fingers clutched in his, and every one was smiling. All went merry as a marriage bell—never had been seen so jovial a way-going.

"Ugh—ugh—ugh!" somebody in the hall suddenly sobbed out from among the white caps of the maids.

"Go upstairs instantly, Jane. Don't disgrace yourself!" cried Janet Sheepshanks sharply, stamping her foot. For the sound of Jane's sudden and shameful collapse sent the other maids' aprons furtively up to their eyes.

And Janet Sheepshanks had no apron. Not that she needed one—of course not.

"Come on, Hugh John—the time is up!" said his father from the side of the dog-cart, where (somewhat ostentatiously) he had been refastening straps which Mike had already done to a nicety.

At this moment Toady Lion passed with half a dozen lettuce leaves. He was no more excited "than nothing at all," as Prissy indignantly said afterwards.

"Good-bye, Toady Lion," said Hugh John, "you can have my other bat and the white rat with the pink eyes."

Toady Lion stood with the lettuce leaves in his arms, looking on in a bored sort of way. Prissy could have slapped him if her hands had not been otherwise employed.

He did not say a word till his brother was perched up aloft on the dog-cart with his cricket bat nursed between his knees and a new hard-hat pulled painfully over his eyes. Then at last Toady Lion spoke. "Did 'oo find the funny fing behind the stable, Hugh John?"

Before Hugh John had time to reply, the dog-cart drove away amid sharp explosions of grief from the white-capped throng. Jane Housemaid dripped sympathy from a first-floor window till the gravel was wet as from a smart shower. Toady Lion alone stood on the steps with his usual expression of bored calmness. Then he turned to Prissy.

"Why is 'oo so moppy?"

"Oh, you go away—you've got no heart!" said Prissy, and resumed her luxury of woe.

If Toady Lion had been a Gallic boy, we should have said that he shrugged his shoulders. At all events, he smiled covertly to the lettuces as he moved off in the direction of the rabbit-hutches.

"It was a very funny fing w'at was behind the stable," he said. For Sir Toady Lion was a humorist. And you can't be a humorist without being a little hard-hearted. Only the heart of a professional writer of pathos can be one degree harder.

CHAPTER XXXVII

THE GOOD CONDUCT PRIZE.

IT was three years after. Sometimes three years makes a considerable change in grown-ups. More often it leaves them pretty much where they were. But with boys and girls the world begins all over again every two years at most. So the terms went and came, and at each vacation, instead of returning home, Hugh John went to London. For it so happened that the year he had left for school the house of Windy Standard was burned down almost to the ground, and Mr. Picton Smith took advantage of the fact to build an entirely new mansion on a somewhat higher site.

The first house might have been saved had the Bounding Brothers been in the neighbourhood, or indeed any active and efficient helpers. But the nearest engine was under the care of the Edam fire brigade, who upon hearing of the conflagration, with great enthusiasm ran their engine a quarter of a mile out of the town by hand. Then their ardour suddenly giving out, they sat down and had an amicable smoke on the roadside till the horse was brought to drag the apparatus the rest of the distance.

But alas! the animal was too fat to be got between the shafts, so it had to be sent back and a leaner horse forwarded. Meantime the house of Windy Standard was blazing merrily, and when the Edam fire company finally arrived, the ashes were still quite hot.

So in this way it came about that it was three long years before Hugh John again saw the hoary battlements of the ancient strength on the castle island which he and his army had attacked so boldly. There were great changes in the town itself. The railway had come to Edam, and now steamed and snorted under the very walls of the Abbey. Chimneys had multiplied, and the smoke columns were taller and denser. The rubicund Provost had gone the way of all the earth, even of all provosts! And the leading bailie, one Donnan, a butcher and army contractor, sat with something less of dignity but equal efficiency in his magisterial chair.

Hugh John from the station platform saw something of this with a sick heart, but he was sure that out in the pure air and infinite quiet of Windy Standard he would find all things the same. But a new and finer house shone white upon the hill. Gardens flourished on unexpected places with that appearance of having been recently planted, frequently pulled up by the roots, looked at and put back, which distinguishes all new gardens. Here and there white-painted vineries and conservatories winked ostentatiously in the sun.

What a time Hugh John had been planning they would have! For months he had thought of nothing but this. Toady Lion and he would do all over again those famous deeds of daring he had done at the castle. Again they would attack the island. Other secret passages would be discovered. All would be as it had been—only nicer. And Cissy Carter—more than everything else he had looked forward to meeting Cissy. Prissy had seen her often, and even during the last week she had written to Hugh John (Prissy always did like to write letters) that Cissy Carter was just splendid—so much older and so improved. Cissy was now nearly seventeen, being (as before) a year and three months older than Hugh John.

Now the distinguished military hero had not been much troubled with sentiment during his school terms. Soldiers at the front never are. He was fully occupied in doing his lessons fairly. He got on well with "the fellows." He was anxious to keep up his end in the games. But, for all that, during these years he had sacredly kept the half of the crooked sixpence in his box, hidden in the end of a tie which he never wore. Now, however, he had looked it out, and by dint of hammering his imagination, he had managed to squeeze out an amount of feeling which quite astonished himself.

He would be noble, generous, forbearing. He remembered how faithfully Cissy had loved him, and how unresponsive he had been in the past. He resolved that all would be very different now.

It was.

Then again he had brought back a record of some distinction from St. Salvator's. He had won the school golf championship. He possessed also a fine bat with an inscription on silver, telling how in the match with St. Aiden's, a rival college of much pretension, he had made 100 not out, and taken eight wickets for sixty-nine.

Besides this presentation cricket bat Hugh John had brought home only one other prize. This was a fitted dressing-bag of beautiful design, with a whole armoury of wonderful silver-plated things inside. It was known as the Good Conduct Prize, and was awarded every year, not by the masters, but by the free votes of all the boys. Prissy was enormously proud of this tribute paid to her brother by his companions. The donor was an old gentleman whose favourite hobby was the promotion of the finer manners of the ancient days, and the terms of the remit on which the award must be made were, that it should be given to the boy who, in the opinion of his fellow-students, was most distinguished for consistent good manners and polite breeding, shown both by his conduct to his superiors in school, and in association with his equals in the playing fields.

At first Hugh John had taken no interest whatever in this award, perhaps from a feeling that his own claims were somewhat slender—or thinking that the prize would merely be some "old book or other." But it happened that, in order to stimulate the school during the last lax and sluggish days of the summer term, the head-master took out the fittings of the dressing-bag, and set the stand containing them on his desk in view of all.

There was a set of razors among them.

Instantly Hugh John's heart yearned with a mighty desire to obtain that prize. How splendid it would be if he could appear at home before Toady Lion and Cissy Carter with a moustache!

That night he considered the matter from all points of view—and felt his muscles. In the morning he was down bright and early. He prowled about the purlieus of the playground. At the back of the gymnasium he met Ashwell Major.

"I say, Ashwell Major," he said, "about that Good Conduct Prize—who are you going to vote for?"

"Well," replied Ashwell Major, "I haven't thought much—I suppose Sammy Carter."

"Oh, humbug!" cried our hero; "see here, Sammy will get tons of prizes anyway. What does he want with that one too?"

"Well," said the other, "let's give it to little Brown. Butter wouldn't melt in his mouth. He's such a cake."

Hugh John felt that the time for moral suasion had come.

"Smell that!" he said, suddenly extending the clenched fist with which a week before he had made "bran mash" of the bully of the school.

"SMELL THAT!"

Reluctantly Ashwell Major's nostrils inhaled the bouquet of Hugh John's knuckles. Ashwell Major seemed to have a dainty and discriminating taste in perfumes, for he did not appear to relish this one.

Then Ashwell Major said that now he was going to vote solidly for Hugh John Smith. He had come to the conclusion that his manners were quite exceptional.

And so as the day went on, did the candidate for the fitted dressing-bag argue with the other boarders, waylaying them one by one as they came out into the playground. The day-boys followed, and each enjoyed the privilege of a smell at the fist of power.

"I rejoice to announce that the Good Conduct Prize has been awarded by the unanimous vote of all the scholars of Saint Salvator's to Hugh John Picton Smith of the fifth form. I am the more pleased with this result, that I have never before known such complete and remarkable unanimity of choice in the long and distinguished history of this institution."

These were the memorable words of the headmaster on the great day of the prize-giving. Whereupon our hero, going up to receive his well-earned distinction, blushed modestly and becomingly; and was gazed upon with wrapt wonder by the matrons and maids assembled, as beyond controversy the model boy of the school. And such a burst of cheering followed him to his seat as had never been heard within the walls of St. Salvator's. For quite casually Hugh John had mentioned that he would be on the look-out for any fellow that was a sneak and didn't cheer like blazes.

Moral.—There is no moral to this chapter.

CHAPTER XXXVIII

HUGH JOHN'S BLIGHTED HEART.

ON the first evening at home Hugh John put on his new straw hat with its becoming school ribbon of brown, white and blue, for he did not forget that Prissy had described Cissy Carter as "such a pretty girl." Now pretty girls are quite nice when they are jolly. What a romp he would have, and even the stile would not be half bad.

He ran down to the landing-stage, having given his old bat and third best fishing-rod to his brother to occupy his attention. Toady Lion was in an unusually adoring frame of mind, chiefly owing to the new bat with the silver inscription which Hugh John had brought home with him. If that were Toady Lion's attitude, how would it be with the enthusiastic Cissy Carter? She must be more than sixteen now. He liked grown-up girls, he thought, so long as they were pretty. And Cissy was pretty, Prissy had distinctly said so.

The white punt bumped against the landing-stage, but the brown was gone. However, he could see it at the other side, swaying against the new pier which Mr. Davenant Carter had built opposite to that of Windy Standard. This was another improvement; you used to have to tie the boat to a bush of bog-myrtle and jump into wet squashy ground. The returned exile sculled over and tied up the punt to an iron ring.

Then with a high and joyous heart he started over the moor, taking the well-beaten path towards Oaklands.

Suddenly, through the wood as it grew thinner and more birchy, he saw the gleam of a white dress. Two girls were walking—no, not two girls, Prissy and a young lady.

"Oh hang!" said Hugh John to himself, "somebody that's stopping with the Carters. She'll go taking up all Cissy's time, and I wanted to see such a lot of her."

The white dresses and summer hats walked composedly on.

"I tell you what," said Hugh John to himself, "I'll scoot through the woods and give them a surprise."

And in five minutes he leaped from a bank into the road immediately before the girls. Prissy gave a little scream, threw up her hands, and then ran eagerly to him.

"Why, Hugh John," she cried, "have you really come? How could you frighten us like that, you bad boy!"

And she kissed him—well, just as Prissy always did.

Meanwhile the young lady had turned partly away, and was pulling carelessly at a leaf—as if such proceedings, if not exactly offensive, were nevertheless highly uninteresting.

"Cissy," called Priscilla at last, "won't you come and shake hands with Hugh John."

The girl turned slowly. She was robed in white linen belted with slim scarlet. The dress came quite down to the tops of her dainty boots. She held out her hand.

"How do you do—ah, Mr. Smith?" she said, with her fingers very much extended indeed.

Hugh John gasped, and for a long moment found no word to say.

"Why, Cissy, how you've grown!" he cried at length. But observing no gleam of fellow-feeling in his quondam comrade's eyes, he added somewhat lamely, "I mean how do you do, Miss— Miss Carter?"

There was silence after this, as the three walked on together, Prissy talking valiantly in order to cover the long and distressful silences. Hugh John's usual bubbling river of speech was frozen upon his lips. He had a thousand things to tell, a thousand thousand to ask. But now it did not seem worth while to speak of one. Why should a young lady like this, with tan gloves half-way to her elbows and the shiniest shoes, with stockings of black silk striped with red, care to hear about his wonderful bat for the three-figure score at cricket, or the fact that he had won the golf medal by doing the round in ninety-five? He had even thought of taking some credit (girls will suck in anything you tell them, you know) for his place in his class, which was seventh. But he had intended to suppress the fact that the fifth form was not a very large one at St. Salvator's.

But now he suddenly became conscious that these trivialities could not possibly interest a young lady who talked about the Hunt Ball in some such fashion as this: "He is such a nice partner, don't you know! He dances—oh, like an angel, and the floor was—well, just perfection!"

Hugh John did not catch the name of this paragon; but he hated the beast anyhow. He did not know that Cissy was only bragging about her bat, and cracking up her score at golf.

"Have you seen 'The White Lady of Avenel' at the Sobriety Theatre, Mr. Smith?" she said, suddenly turning to him.

"No," grunted Hugh John, "but I've seen the Drury Lane pantomime. It was prime!"

The next moment he was sorry he had said it. But the truth slipped out before he knew. For so little was Hugh John used to the society of grown-up big girls, that he did not know any better than to tell them the truth.

"Ah, yes!" commented Cissy Carter condescendingly, "I used quite to like going to pantomimes when I was a child!"

A slight and elegant young man, with a curling moustache turned up at the ends, came towards them down the bank. He had grey-and-white striped trousers on, a dark cutaway coat, and a smart straw hat set on the back of his head. He wore gloves and walked with a pretty cane. Hugh John loathed him on sight.

"Good-evening, Courtenay," said Cissy familiarly, "this is my friend, Prissy Smith, of whom you have heard me speak; and this is her brother just home from school!"

("What a beast! I hate him! Calls that a moustache, I daresay. Ha, ha! he should just see Ashwell Major's. And I can lick Ashwell Major with one hand!")

"Aw," said the young man with the cane, superciliously stroking his maligned upper lip, "the preparatory school, I daresay—Lord, was at one once myself—beastly hole!"

("I don't doubt it, you look it," was Hugh John's mental note.) Aloud he said, "Saint Salvator's is a ripping place. We beat Glen Fetto by an innings and ninety-one!"

Mr. Courtenay Carling took no notice. He was talking earnestly and confidentially to his cousin. Hugh John had had enough of this.

"Come on, Priss," he said roughly, "let's go home."

Prissy was nothing loath. She was just aching to get him by himself, so that she might begin to burn incense at his manly shrine. She had had stacks of it ready, and the match laid for weeks and weeks.

"Good-night," said Cissy frigidly. Hugh John took hold of her dainty gloved fingers as gingerly as if each had been a stinging nettle, and dropped them as quickly. Mr. Courtenay Carling paused in his conversation just long enough to say over his shoulder, "Ah—ta-ta—got lots of pets to run round and see, I s'pose—rabbits and guinea-pigs; used to keep 'em myself, you know, beastly things, ta-ta!"

And with Cissy by his side he moved off, alternately twirling his moustache and glancing approvingly down at her. Cissy on her part never once looked round, but kept poking her parasol into the plants at the side of the road, as determinedly as if it had been the old pike manufactured by the exiled king O'Donowitch. Such treatment could not have been at all good for such a miracle of silk and lace and cane; but somehow its owner did not seem to mind.

"What an awful brute!" burst out Hugh John, as soon as Prissy and he were clear.

"Oh, how can you say so!" said Prissy, much surprised; "why, every one thinks him so nice. He has such lots of money, and is going to stand for Parliament—that is, if his uncle would only die, or have something happen to him!"

Her brother snorted, as if to convey his contempt for "everybody's" opinion on such a matter; but Prissy was too happy to care for aught save the fact that once more her dear Hugh John was safe at home.

"Do you know," she said lovingly, "I could not sleep last night for thinking of your coming! It is so splendid. There's the loveliest lot of roses being planted in the new potting house, and I've got a pearl necklace to show you—such a beauty—and——"

Thus she rattled on, joyously ticking off all the things she had to show him. She ran a little ahead to look at him, then ran as quickly back to hug him. "Oh, you dear!" she exclaimed. And all the while the heart of the former valiant soldier sank deep and ever deeper into the split-new cricketing shoes he had been so proud of when he sallied forth to meet Cissy Carter by the stile.

"Come on," she cried presently, picking up her skirts. "I'm so excited I don't know what to do. I can't keep quiet. I believe I can race you yet, for all you're so big and have won a silver cricket bat. How I shall love to see it! Come on, Hugh John, I'll race you to the gipsy camp for a pound of candy!"

But Hugh John did not want to race. He did not want not to race. He did not want ever to do anything any more—only to fade away and die. His heart was cold and dead within him. He felt that he would never know happiness again. But he could not bear to disappoint Prissy the first night. Besides, he could easily enough beat her—he was sure of that. So he smiled indulgently and nodded acquiescence. He had not told her that he had won the school mile handicap from scratch.

They started, and Hugh John began to run scientifically, as he had been taught to do at school, keeping a little behind Prissy, ready to spurt at the last and win by a neck. Doubtless this would have answered splendidly, only that Prissy ran so fast. She did not know anything about scientific sprinting, but she could run like the wind. So by the time they reached the Partan Burn she had completely outclassed Hugh John. With her skirts held high in her hand over she flew like a bird; but her brother, jumping the least bit too soon, went splash into the shallows, sending the water ten feet into the air.

Like a shot Prissy was back, and reached a hand down to the vanquished scientific athlete.

"Oh, I'm so sorry, Hugh John," she said; "I ought to have told you it had been widened. Don't let's race any more. I think I must have started too soon, and you'd have beaten me anyway. Here's the gipsy camp."

The world-weary exile looked about him. He had thought that at least it might be some manly pleasure to see Billy Blythe once more, and try a round with the Bounding Brothers. After all, what did it matter about girls? He had a twelve-bladed knife in his pocket which he intended for Billy, and he knew a trick of boxing—a feint with the right, and then an upward blow with the left, which he knew would interest his friend.

But the tents were gone. The place where they had stood was green and unencumbered. Only an aged crone or two moved slowly about among the small thatched cottages. To one of these Hugh John addressed himself.

"Eh, master—Billy Blythe—why, he be 'listed for a sodger—a corp'ral they say he be, and may be sergeant by this time, shouldn't wonder. Eh, dearie, and the Boundin' Brothers—oh! ye mean the joompin' lads. They're off wi' a circus in Ireland. Nowt left but me and my owd mon! Thank ye, sir, you be a gentleman born, as anybody can see without the crossin' o' the hand."

Sadly Hugh John moved away, a still more blighted being. He left Prissy at the white lodge-gate in order that she might go home to meet Mr. Picton Smith on his return from the county town, where he had been judging the horses at an agricultural show. He would take a walk through the town, he said to himself, and perhaps he might meet some of his old enemies. He felt that above everything he would enjoy a sharp tussle. After all what save valour was worth living for? Wait till he was a soldier, and came back in uniform with a sword by his side and the scar of a wound on his forehead—would Cissy Carter despise him then? He would show her! In the meantime he had learned certain tricks of fence which he would rather like to prove on the countenances of his former foes.

So with renewed hope in his heart he took his way through the town of Edam. The lamps were just being lighted, and Hugh John lounged along through the early dusk with his hands in his pockets, looking out for a cause of offence. Presently he came upon a brilliantly lighted building, into which young men and women were entering singly and in pairs.

A hanging lamp shone down upon a noticeboard. He had nothing better to do. He stopped and read—

Edam Mutual Improvement Society.
SEASON 18—
Hon. President.—Rev. Mr. Burnham.
Hon. Vice-President.—Mr. N. Donnan.
Hon. Sec. and Treasurer.—Mr. Nathaniel Cuthbertson.
DEBATE TO-NIGHT.

Subject.—"Is the Pen mightier than the Sword?"
Affirmative.—Mr. N. Donnan.
Negative.—Mr. Burnham.
All are Cordially Invited.
Bring your Hymn-books.

Hugh John did not accept the invitation, perhaps because he had no hymn-book. He only waited outside to hear Mr. N. Donnan's opening sentence. It ran thus: "All ages of the world's history have borne testimony to the fact that peace is preferable to war, right to might, and the sweet still voice of Reason to the savage compulsions of brutal Force."

"Oh, hang!" ejaculated Hugh John, doubling his fist; "did you ever hear such rot? I wish I could jolly well fetch Nipper Donnan one on the nob!"

And he sauntered on till he came to the burying-ground of Edam's ancient abbey. He wandered aimlessly up the short avenue, stood at the gate a while, then kicked it open and went in. He clambered about among the graves, stumbling over the grassy mounds till he came to the tombs of his ancestors. At least they were not quite his ancestors, but the principle was the same. "There's nothing exclusive about me. I'll adopt them," said Hugh John to himself, as many another distinguished person had done before him. They were in fact the tombs of the Lorraines, the ancient possessors and original architects of the Castle of Windy Standard, which he had spilt his best blood to defend. Well, it was to attack. But no matter.

He sat down and looked at the defaced and battered tombs in silence. Mighty thoughts coursed through his brain. His heart was filled full to the brim with the sadness of mortality. Tears of hopeless resignation stood in his eyes. It was the end, the solemn end of all. Soon he, too, like them, would be lying low and quiet. He began to be conscious of a general fatal weakness of the system, a hollowness of the chest (or stomach), which showed that the end was near.

Ah, they would be sorry then—she would be sorry! And after morning service in church, they would come and stand by his grave and say—she would say, "He was young, but he lived nobly, though, alas! there was none to appreciate him. Ah, would that he were again alive!" Then they (she) would weep, yes, weep bitterly, and fling themselves (herself) upon the cold, cold ground. But all in vain. He (Hugh John Picton Smith, late hero) would lie still in death under that green sod and never say a word. No, not even if he could. Like Brer Fox, he would lie low. At this point Hugh John was so moved that he put his face down into his hands and sobbed.

A heavy clod of earth whizzed through the air and impacted itself with a thud upon the mourner's cheek, filling his ear with mud and sand, and informing him at the same instant that it carried a stone concealed somewhere about its person.

For though Nipper Donnan was now Vice-President of a Mutual Improvement Association, and at that moment spreading himself in a peroration upon the advantages of universal goody-goodiness, he had, happily for society and Hugh John, left exceedingly capable successors. The eternal Smoutchy was still very much alive, and still an amateur of clods in the town of Edam.

That sod worked a complete and sudden cure in Hugh John.

He rose like a shot. Few and short were the prayers he said, but what these petitions lacked in length they made up for in fervency. He pursued his assailant down the Mill Brae, clamoured after him round the Town-yards, finally cornered him at the Spital Port, punched his head soundly—and felt better.

So that night the unfortunate young martyr to the flouts and scorns of love, instead of occupying a clay-cold bier with his (adopted) ancestors in Edam Abbey graveyard, ate an excellent supper in the new house of Windy Standard, with three helpings of round-of-beef and vegetables to match. Then with an empty heart, but a full stomach, he betook himself upstairs to his room, where presently Toady Lion came to worship, and Prissy dropped in to see that all was well. She had spread prettily worked covers of pink silk over his brushes and combs, an arrangement which the hero contemplated with disgust.

He seized them, gathered them into a knot, and flung them into a corner.

"Oh, Hugh John!" cried Prissy, "how could you? And they took such a long time to do!"

And there were the premonitions of April showers in the sensitive barometer of Priscilla's eyes.

The brother was touched—as much, that is, as it is in the nature of a brother to be. But in the interests of discipline he could not give way too completely.

"All right, Prissy," he said, "it was no end good of you. But really, you know, a fellow couldn't be expected to put up with these things. Why, they'd stick in your nails and tangle up all your traps so that you'd wish you were dead ten times a day, or else they'd make you say 'Hang!' and things."

"Very well," said Prissy, with sweetest resignation, "then I will take them for myself, but I did think you would have liked them!"

"Did you, Priss—you are a good sort!" said Hugh John, patting his sister on the cheek.

His sister felt that after such a demonstration of affection from him there was little left to live for.

"Good-night, you dear," she said; "I'll wake you in the morning, and have your bath ready for you at eight."

"Good old girl!" said Hugh John tolerantly, and went to bed, glad that he had been so nice to Prissy about the brush-covers. Such a little makes a girl happy, you know.

Perhaps, all things being considered, it was for the good of our hero's soul at this time that Cissy Carter was on hand to take some of the conceit out of him.

CHAPTER XXXIX

"GIRLS ARE FUNNY THINGS."

GIRLS are funny things" was Hugh John's favourite maxim; and he forthwith proceeded to prove that boys are too, by making a point of seeing Cissy Carter several times a week during his entire vacation. Yet he was unhappy as often as he went to Oaklands, and only more unhappy when he stayed away. On the whole, Cissy was much less frigid than on that first memorable evening. But she never thawed entirely, nor could Hugh John discover the least trace of the hair-brained madcap of ancient days for whom his whole soul longed, in the charmingly attired young lady whose talk and appearance were so much beyond her years. But he shaved three or four times a day with his new razors, sneaking hot water on the sly in order to catch up.

The last time he could hope to see her before going back to school for his final term, was on the evening of a day when Hugh John had successfully captained a team of schoolboys and visitors from the surrounding country-houses against the best eleven which Edam could produce. Cissy Carter had looked on with Mr. Courtenay Carling by her side, while Captain (once General Napoleon) Smith made seventy-seven, and carried out his still virgin bat amid the cheers of the spectators, after having beaten the Edamites by four wickets, and with only six minutes to spare in order to save the draw.

"Oh, well played!" cried Mr. Carling patronisingly, as Hugh John came up, modestly swinging his bat as if he did as much every day of his life; "I remember when I was at the 'Varsity——"

But Hugh John turned away without waiting to hear what happened to Mr. Carling at the 'Varsity which he had honoured with his presence. It chanced, however, that at that moment the young gentleman with the moustache saw on the other side of the enclosure a lady of more mature charms than those of his present companion, whose father also had a great deal of influence—don't you know?—in the county. So in a little while he excused himself and went over to talk with his new friend in her carriage, afterwards driving home with her to "a quiet family dinner."

Thus Cissy was left to return alone with Sammy, and she gathered up her sunshade and gloves with an air of calm and surprising dignity. Hugh John had meant to bid her an equally cool good night and stroll off with the worshipful Toady Lion—who that day had kept wickets "like a jolly little brick" (as his brother was good enough to say), besides making a useful six before being run out. But somehow, when the hero of the day went to say good-bye, he could not quite carry out his programme, and found himself, against his will, offering in due form to "see Miss Carter home."

Which shows that Hugh John, like his moustache, was growing up very rapidly indeed, and learning how to adapt himself to circumstances. He wondered what Ashwell Major would say if he knew. It would make him sick, Hugh John thought; but after all, what was a fellow to do?

For the first mile they talked freely about the match, and Cissy complimented him on his scoring. Then there fell a silence and constraint upon them. They were approaching the historic stile. Hugh John nerved himself for a daring venture.

"Do you remember what you once made me say here, Cissy?" he said. Miss Carter turned upon him a perfectly well-bred stare of blankest ignorance.

"No," she said, "I don't remember ever being here with you before."

"Oh, come, no humbug, Cissy—you could remember very well if you wanted to," said Hugh John roughly. As he would have described it himself, "his monkey was getting up. Cissy had better look out."

He took from his ticket-pocket the piece of the crooked sixpence, which he had kept for more than three years in his schoolbox. "You don't remember that either, I suppose?" he said with grave irony.

Cissy looked at the broken coin calmly—she would have given a great deal if she had had a pincenez or a quizzing-glass to put up at that point. But she did her best without either. Strangely, however, Hugh John was not even irritated.

"No," she said at last, "it looks like half of a sixpence which somebody has stepped upon. How quaint! Did you find it, or did some one give it to you?"

They were at the stile now, and Hugh John helped Cissy over. The grown-up swing of her skirt as she tripped down was masterly. It looked so natural. On the other side they both stopped, faced about, and set their elbows on the top almost as they had done three or four years ago when—but so much had happened since then.

With even more serenity Hugh John took a small purse out of his pocket. It was exceedingly dusty, as well it might be, for he had picked it out from underneath the specially constructed grandstand at the cricket ground. He opened it quietly, in spite of the unladylike snatch which Cissy made as soon as she recognised it, dropping her youngladyish hauteur in an instant. Hugh John held the dainty purse high up out of her reach, and extracted from an inner compartment a small piece of silver.

"IT LOOKS LIKE HALF OF A SIXPENCE WHICH SOMEBODY HAS STEPPED UPON. HOW QUAINT!"

"Give it back to me this moment," cried Cissy, who had lost all her reserve, and suddenly grown whole years younger. "I didn't think any one in the world could be so mean. But I might have known. Do you hear—give it back to me, Hugh John."

With the utmost deliberation he snapped the catch and handed her the purse. The bit of silver he fitted carefully to the first piece he had taken from his ticket-pocket and held them up. They were the reunited halves of the same crooked sixpence.

Then he looked at Cissy with some of her own former calmness.

He even offered her the second fragment of silver, whereupon with a sudden petulant gesture she struck his hand up, and her own half of the crooked sixpence flew into the air, flashed once in the rays of the setting sun, and fell in the middle of the path.

Hugh John stood in front of her a moment silent. Then he spoke.

"Do you know, Cissy, you are a regular little fraud!"

And with that he suddenly caught the girl in his arms, kissed her once, twice, thrice—and then sprang over the stile, and down towards the river almost as swiftly as Prissy herself. The girl stood a moment speechless with surprise and indignation. Then the tears leaped to her eyes, and she stamped her foot.

"Oh, I hate you, I despise you!" she cried, putting all her injured pride and anger into the indignant ring of her voice. "I'll never speak to you again—not as long as I live, Hugh John Smith!"

And she turned away homeward, holding her head very high in the air. She seemed to be biting her lips to keep back the tears which threatened to overflow her cheeks. But just as she was leaving the stile, curiously enough she cast sharply over her shoulder and all round her the quick shy look of a startled fawn—and stooped to the path. The next moment the bit of silver which had sparkled there was gone, and Cissy Carter, with eyes still moist, but with the sweetest and most wistful smile playing upon her face, was tripping homeward to Oaklands to the tune of "The Girl I left behind me," which she liked to whistle softly when she was sure no one was listening.

And at the end of every verse she gave a little skip, as if her heart were light within her.

Girls are funny things.

Transcriber's note:

Inconsistent and archaic spelling, syntax, and punctuation retained.

Printed in Great Britain
by Amazon